GYMNASTIC ACTIVITIES • DA

CW00497358

PE LESSON PLANS

year 4

COMPLETE TEACHING PROGRAMME

SECOND EDITION

LEAPFROGS

JIM HALL

A music CD with tracks to accompany many of the Dance Lessons in this series is available separately (ISBN: 978 07136 7902 1)

Relevant tracks are indicated on each lesson page with the following logo:

Published in 2009 by A & C Black Publishers Ltd,
an imprint of Bloomsbury Publishing Plc
50 Bedford Square, London, WC1B 3DP
www.bloomsbury.com

Second edition, 2009; reprinted 2012

ISBN 978 14081 0993 9

A CIP record for this book is available from the British Library.

Note: While every effort has been made to ensure that the content of this book is as technically accurate and as sound as possible, neither the author nor the publisher can accept responsibility for any injury or loss sustained as a result of the use of this material.

A & C Black uses paper produced with elemental chlorine-free pulp, harvested from managed sustainable forests.

Acknowledgements
Cover illustration by Tom Croft
Cover design by James Watson
Illustrations by Jan Smith

Typeset in 10pt DIN Regular.

Printed and bound in Croatia by Zrinski.

Contents

Introduction

Because an increasing number of young children today do not have the opportunity to take part in regular play, physical activity or exercise, enjoyable, vigorous, well taught physical education lessons are more important than ever. Equally important is a sense of staff unity regarding the 'Why?', the 'What?', and the 'How?' of physical education to deliver a whole school, successful programme with continuity and high standards from year to year. The main reasons for teaching physical education, include:

Physical development. First and foremost, the main reason for teaching physical education has always been to inspire vigorous, enjoyable, challenging and wholehearted physical activity that develops normal healthy growth and satisfactory development of each pupil's strength, suppleness and stamina. The skills taught also aim to develop skilful, confident, well-controlled and safe movement. It is hoped that the varied skills will give pleasure and satisfaction, catering for many interests and aptitudes, and will eventually enable pupils to take part in healthy, worthwhile and sociable activities long after they have left school. These skills, learned and enjoyed at school, are remembered by the body for a very long time.

Personal, social and emotional development, compensating for the near total disappearance of play in the out-of-school lives of many of our pupils. It is reported that millions of children spend most of their free time – up to five hours every day – watching a TV or a computer screen. It has also been claimed that parents, who refuse to let their children go out to play, are producing a 'battery-farmed' generation who will never become resilient and will be unable to deal with risk.

This lack of play means no exercise, no fresh air, no physical development, no social development though interaction with others, no adventure in challenging situations and no emotional development. It has been said 'an individual's regard for, and attitude to, his or her physical self, especially at primary school age, is important to the development of self-image and the value given to self.' Physical education lessons are extremely visual, providing many opportunities for demonstrating success, creativity, versatility and enthusiastic performances which should be recognised by the teacher, praised and commented upon, and shared with others who should be encouraged to be warm in their praise and comments. Such successes can enhance a pupil's feelings of pride and self-confidence.

The play-like nature of physical education lessons is obvious. In games, running, jumping and landing, throwing and catching, batting, skipping, trying to score points or goals; in gymnastic activities, running, jumping and landing, rolling, climbing, swinging on ropes, balancing, circling on bars; and in dance, skipping, running and jumping, travelling with a partner, a group or a circle in performing a dance, are all playful actions in which pupils find fun and satisfaction from performing well, and social development from being in the company of others.

When teaching physical education lessons now, teachers need to remember that the lessons may be providing the only active play that some of the pupils will experience that week. The lessons must be vigorous, enjoyable, and give an impression of children at play.

Contributing to pupils' health now, and long after they have left school. The health of our children and eventually the health of our nation, has been a cause for concern for university researchers and health experts for decades. A 1997 headline described British children as 'The Flab Generation'. It was estimated in 2000, that in a class of thirty children, two will go on to have a heart attack, three will develop diabetes, and thirteen will become obese, all as result of a sedentary lifestyle and a diet dominated by chips, biscuits, sweets and sugary drinks. A 2002 report revealed that a third of 10 year olds did not even walk continuously for ten minutes a week.

The above statistics and figures have become far worse since those early ignored warnings. The NHS treated 85,000 patients for clinical obesity in 2007 and a 2008 report from the NHS Information Centre claims that 'a third of children between the ages of 2 and 15 are now obese or overweight'. England has the fastest growing weight problem in Europe. The link between obesity and diabetes is well known and 100,000 UK patients are diagnosed with type 2 diabetes every year, fuelled by the nation's obesity problem. Douglas Smallwood, Chief Executive of the charity Diabetes UK says 'Diabetes is a serious condition which can lead to devastating complications such as blindness, amputation, heart and kidney disease.' Almost one hundred diabetics a week have a limb amputated because of complications with their disease.

An extra twelve kilograms in weight boosts the risk of cancer by 50%. Coronary heart disease causes 105,000 deaths a year and 2.6 million people are thought to be living with the symptoms of heart disease. Scientists have warned that unfit, lazy children are six times more likely to develop early signs of heart disease than those who are active and take exercise. For the first time, experts have established that activity levels in children as young as seven can have a serious effect on their future health. Professor Paul Gately, of Leeds Metropolitan University says 'Inactive children at a relatively young age are already storing up health risks for the future.' Health specialists, concerned for the health of our nation, are now repeatedly emphasising the importance of regular exercise as the best way to reduce the risks of suffering life-threatening illnesses in later life.

The National Obesity Forum has called for urgent action to tackle the obesity problem which, they calculate, causes 30,000 deaths each year and emphasises that the time to act is in childhood before irreversible damage has been done, and while lifelong habits can be learned. British Heart Foundation research found that taking 30 minutes of moderate exercise most days reduces the risk of an early death by more than a quarter. Diabetes UK warns that obesity is making a diabetes epidemic inevitable. Physical activity and a sensible diet are the best ways to reduce the risk of developing diabetes. The World Cancer Research Fund 2007 Report, produced by scientists and medical experts from around the world, tells us that most cancers are preventable by choosing a healthy diet, being physically active and maintaining a healthy weight. They recommend being physically active for at least 30 minutes every day, to keep the heart healthy and to reduce the risk of cancer.

Realistically, it is only in schools in physical education lessons, that we can encourage and help children to succeed in a wide range of physical skills and inspire, motivate and facilitate a joy in physical activity that will combat the health problems mentioned above. Physical education makes a unique contribution to an all-round, balanced education, but it also makes a special contribution to a life-prolonging, healthy lifestyle. For today's primary school children regular, excellent, vigorous and enjoyable physical education lessons are probably the best health products they will ever receive.

Teaching Physical Education

The teacher of physical education, almost uniquely, works alone and unaided, and is involved in whole class teaching with no help from the mass of teaching aids that help to keep pupils purposefully and often independently engaged in their classrooms. Even if he or she is talking to an individual, a pair or a small group, the teacher in a physical education lesson still needs to be aware of the whole class and how it is responding to the set task.

The teacher is the source and inspiration for everything that happens in the lessons. He or she needs to be well prepared to make the lesson complete, enjoyable, stimulating and challenging; enthusiastic to create an equally enthusiastic response; warm and encouraging to help pupils feel pleased and good about themselves; and intensely interested in inspiring vigorous physical activity in pupils, many of whom, away from school, may have inactive and sedentary lifestyles.

The lesson plan is the teacher's essential guide and reminder of the current lesson's content. Failure to plan and record lessons results in the same or similar things being done, month after month. Parts of the lesson gradually disappear, and an unprepared teacher can finish up doing no teaching in a lesson where everything is vague or has been done before. Pupils at apparatus in such an unprepared lesson answer 'Nothing' when asked 'What has your group been asked to do at this apparatus?'

July's lesson will only be at a more advanced stage that the previous September's if all the lessons in between have been recorded and referred to, to make each succeeding lesson move on and introduce new, interesting and exciting challenges. The lesson usually runs for four or five weeks (one lesson per week) to give the class enough time to practise, improve, develop, learn, remember and enjoy all the skills involved.

'Dead spots' and queue avoidance. The 'scenes of busy activity' which every physical education lesson should be requires an understanding by all pupils that they should be 'found working, not waiting'. This means that they need to be trained to respond immediately, behave well, keep on practising until stopped, and avoid standing immobile in queues.

The teacher needs to avoid talking the class out of their lesson through over-long explanations, demonstrations and pupil reflections following demonstrations. Lessons that lose a lot of time result in unsatisfactory, hurried apparatus work, frustratingly short time for playing games, and half-created dances with no time to share them proudly, with the class.

Demonstrations and observations by pupils and teacher are essential teaching aids because we remember what we see – good quality work; safe, correct ways to perform; the exact meanings of physical education terminology; and good examples of variety and interesting contrasts. All can watch one, two or a small group. Half of the class can watch the other half. Each can watch a partner. These occasional demonstrations, with comments by the observing pupils, often bring out good points not noticed by the teacher; train pupils to understand the elements of 'movement'; and let teachers ask 'how can it be improved?' Making friendly, encouraging, helpful points to classmates is good for class morale and for extending the class repertoire in physical education. ('Occasional' means once or twice at most in one lesson because of the time taken to do this.)

Further class practice should always follow a demonstration so that everyone can try to include some of the good features praised and commented on.

Shared choice or **indirect teaching** takes place when the teacher decides the nature of the activity and challenges the class to decide on the actions. Limits set are determined by the experience of the pupils. From the simple 'Can you travel on the apparatus, using your hands and feet?' with its slight limitations, we can progress on to 'Can you travel on the apparatus, using hands and feet, and include a still balance, a direction change, and taking all the weight on your hands at some point?'

Shared choice teaching produces a wide variety of results to add to the class repertoire. Being creative is extremely satisfying and most primary school pupils enjoy and are capable of making individual responses.

Direct teaching takes place when the teacher tells the class what to do, including, for example: any of the traditional gymnastic skills; the way to hold, throw and catch a ball; or how to do a folk dance step. Correct, safe ways to move; support yourself; grip, lift and carry apparatus; and throw implements, are all directly taught.

If the class is restless, not responding, or doing poor work, a directed activity can restore interest and discipline and provide ideas and a valuable starting point from which to develop. Pupils who are less interested, less inventive or less gifted physically, will benefit from direct teaching, particularly if the teacher can suggest an alternative, simpler but equally acceptable idea. 'If you do not like rolling forwards, try rolling sideways instead. Start, curled up on your back, with your hands clasped under your knees. This keeps your head out of the way.' The occasional stimulus of a direct request is the kind of challenge many pupils enjoy, and they respond enthusiastically. 'Can you and your partner bat the small ball up and down between you, six times?'

Motivational teaching. Children say that the things that motivate them to take part in physical activities are fun and skill development. They want to enjoy, learn and succeed. The more philosophical among them might also add that feelings of happiness are associated with having something to look forward to; to enjoy; and then to remember with pleasure (and often with pride). This anticipation, realisation and retrospect-inspiring potential of excellent physical education lessons and activities, makes it the favourite subject for many primary school pupils.

Safe Practice and Accident Prevention

In physical education lessons, where a main aim is to contribute to normal, healthy growth and physical development, we must do everything possible to avoid accidents.

Good supervision by the teacher is key to safe practice. He or she must be there with the class at all times, and teaching from positions from which the majority of the class can be seen. This usually means circulating on the outside looking in, with no-one behind his or her back. Good teaching develops skilful, well-controlled, safe movement with pupils wanting to avoid others to ensure that they have space to practise and perform well and not be impeded in any way. The outward expression of this caring attitude we are trying to create is the sensible, unselfish sharing of hall floor space, apparatus and playground, and self-control in avoiding others.

Badly behaved classes who do not respond immediately, or start or stop as requested; who rush around selfishly and noisily disturbing others; who are never quiet in their tongues or body movements; and who do not try to move well, are destructive of any prospects for high standards or lesson enjoyment by the majority and the teacher. A safe environment requires a well-behaved, quiet, attentive and responsive class. Good behaviour must be continually pursued until it becomes the normal, expected way to work in every lesson. There is nothing to talk about, apart from those occasions when comments are requested after a demonstration, or when partners are quietly discussing their response to a challenge.

The hall should be at a good working temperature with windows and doors opened or closed to cope with changing seasons and central heating variations. Potentially dangerous chairs, tables, trolleys, piano or television should be removed or pushed against a wall or into a corner. Floor sockets for receiving securing pins for ropes and climbing frames should be regularly cleared of cleaning substances which harden and block the small sockets.

In playground games lessons, pupils must be trained to remain inside the lines of the grids or netball courts and to avoid running, chasing or dodging into fences, walls, sheds, seats, hutted classrooms, or steps into buildings. In any 'tag' games, pupils must be told 'Touch the person you have caught very gently, never pushing them or causing them to fall or stumble.'

Before the lesson, the teacher checks for sensible, safe clothing with no watches, rings or jewellery whose impact against another child can cause serious scarring or injury; no long trousers that catch heels; no long sleeves that catch thumbs, impeding safe gripping; and no long, un-bunched hair that impedes vision. Indoors, barefoot work is recommended because it is quiet, provides a safe, strong grip on apparatus, enhances the appearance of the work, and enables the little-used muscles of feet and ankles to develop as they grip, balance, support, propel and receive the body weight.

In teaching gymnastic activities, the following safety considerations are important:

○ In floor and apparatus work, pupils need to be taught the correct, safe, 'squashy' landing after a jump so that they land safely on the balls of the feet, with ankles, knees and hips 'giving' without jarring.

○ When inverted, with all the weight on their hands, pupils need to be taught to keep fingers pointing forward, arms straight and strong, and head looking forward, not back under arms. Looking back under the arms makes every-thing appear to be upside down.

○ On climbing frames, pupils must be told 'Fingers grip over the bar, thumbs grip under the bar, always, for a safe, strong grip.'

A Suggested Way to Start a First Lesson With a New Class

Unless taught otherwise, pupils travel round the hall or the playground in an anti-clockwise circle, all following the person in front of them. If one pupil slows down or stops suddenly, the next can bump into that person, possible knocking him or her over, causing an angry upset and a disturbance.

By travelling and confining themselves within this circle, a class fails to use all the possible room or playground space, depriving themselves of enough space to travel freely in different directions, and to join several actions together, on the spot or travelling about. Also, with everyone travelling round in a circle, sometimes side by side, pairs of less well-behaved pupils can be so close together that their poor behaviour, expressed in talking, not listening, slow responses, and noisy, poor performances, completely upsets the teacher's aim to give the class an enjoyable, lively, quiet, thoughtful and co-operative start to the lesson and the year's programme.

By continually making the whole class listen for the signal 'Stop!', we force them to pay attention, listen, and respond quickly.

Suggested pre-start to the lesson

1 Please show me your very best walking...go! Visit every part of the room, the sides, the ends, corners, as well as the middle. Swing your arms strongly and step out smartly.

2 When I call 'Stop!', show me how quickly you can stop and stand perfectly still. Keep walking smartly and visiting all parts of the room. Stop! Stand still!

3 If you are standing too near a piece of apparatus, like Liam by the piano, or too near someone else, like Thomas and Emily, please take one step into a big space all by yourself. Go!

4 When you start walking this time, travel along straight lines, never following anyone. If you find yourself behind someone, change direction and continue along a new straight line, following no-one. Ready? Go!

5 Come on. March briskly and smartly and pretend you are leaving footprints in every part of the room. When I call 'Stop!' you will stop immediately and then take a step into your own space if you are near apparatus or another person. Stop!

6 In our next practice, listen for my 'Stop!' and show me that no-one is standing behind another person, looking towards that person's back, following them. Go!

7 Stop! Stand still, after moving onto your own space if necessary. Now show your very best running, with the emphasis on lifting your heels, knees and hands to keep your running soft, silent and strong – and, of course, travelling along straight lines, never following anyone.

8 Stop! Be still! This half of the class stand with feet apart, arms folded, to watch this other half doing their very best running. Look out for and tell me later about anyone whose running you liked and be able to tell me what you liked about it. The running half...ready...go! Do not pick anyone who is following someone, or anyone who is not lifting heels, knees or arms strongly. Please watch carefully.

9 Stop! Watchers, whose running did you like. Yes, Daniel?

10 I (Daniel) liked Kate's running because she used her eyes well, looking for spaces, and she seemed to float along beautifully and easily, with heels, knees and hands being lifted high.

11 Thank you very much, Daniel, for that excellent answer. Now let's look at Kate to see and learn from the good things mentioned by Daniel. Please run again, Kate.

12 (Repeat with the other half working and the other half observing and commenting.)

Potential Cross-Curricular Outcomes of Physical Education Lessons for Juniors

Language Many teachers recognise the valuable contribution that physical education lessons can make to language development and a clearer understanding of the meanings of words. Hearing, reading and writing are the usual relationships between pupils and words. In physical education lessons, pupils do, experience and feel the action words concerned. Clear demonstrations by the teacher or a pupil also lead to a greater understanding of the exact meanings of action words.

In Year 3, Games Lesson 2, for example, there are: run, side-step, avoid, count, touch, walk, throw, catch, bounce, receive, pass, move, invent, develop, advance, change, practise, revise, show and skip. Jog, sprint, bowl, dodge, mark, chase, aim, reach, land, dribble and receive are also frequently used in games lessons.

In a typical gymnastic activities lesson, pupils will also experience, understand and feel the meanings of the many prepositions used, for example, in Year 4, Lesson 3: over, through, on, astride, along, upward, off, across, up to, from, near, away. Beside, beneath, towards, around, are also used frequently in gymnastics lessons.

Adverbs describe the quality or degree of effort in an action as in Year 5, Dance Lesson 9: vigorously, firmly, slowly, lively, lightly, loosely, stiffly, clearly and loudly. Quickly, gently, strongly, smoothly, suddenly, silently, smartly, carefully, splendidly and explosively, are also used frequently in dance lessons.

Writing Still within language, pupils can be challenged to complete 'The part(s) of the gymnastics lesson where I felt (choose one of) for example, excited, pleased, surprised, tired, proud, anxious, hot, breathless, strong, stretched, sociable, unsure, relaxed, was/were...' They can be asked to try to explain why they were experiencing the feelings that they listed.

A mountaineer once said 'When I climb, I can feel life effervescing within me.' A pupil who has just completed a rope climb for the first time; or done a beautifully controlled handstand, then lowered into a forward roll; or completed their own created dance or gymnastic sequence with complete control from start to finish, with attractive use of space and effort; or outwitted a close marking opponent, before going on to score, will be experiencing intense excitement, pride and pleasure, deserving of the opportunity to try to produce an eloquent expression about what might have been an unforgettable event.

Art They can be asked 'Can you draw the gymnastic action or actions that gave you the most pleasure or excitement in today's lesson? Under your heading, can you explain in a few words why you were pleased or excited?'

Physical Education can also contribute to pupils':

- **spiritual development** through helping them gain a sense of achievement and develop positive attitudes towards themselves

- **moral development** through helping pupils gain a sense of fair play based on rules and the conventions of activities; and develop positive sporting behaviour, knowing how to conduct themselves in sporting competition

- **social development** through helping pupils develop social skills in activities involving co-operation and collaboration, responsibility, personal commitment, loyalty and teamwork, and considering the social importance of physical activity, sport and dance.

Gymnastic Activities

Introduction to Gymnastic Activities

Gymnastic Activities is the indoor lesson that includes varied floorwork on a clear floor, unimpeded by apparatus, followed by varied apparatus work which should take up just over half of the lesson time. Ideally, the portable apparatus will have been positioned around the sides and ends of the room, near to where it will be used, before lessons start in the morning or afternoon. This allows each of the seven or eight mixed infant groups, or the five or six mixed junior groups of pupils to lift, carry and position their apparatus in a very short time, because no set will need to be moved more than 3–5 metres. The lesson is traditionally of 30 minutes duration.

The following pages aim, first of all, to produce a sense of staff-room unity regarding the nature of good practice and high standards in teaching Gymnastic Activities lessons. Without this sense of unity among the teachers concerned, there is no continuity of aims, expectations or programme, and there will be a less than satisfactory level of achievement. Secondly, the following pages provide a full scheme of work for Gymnastic Activities. There is a lesson plan and accompanying pages of detailed explanatory notes for every month, designed to help teachers and schools with ideas for lessons that are progressive.

Why We Teach Gymnastic Activities

Ideally, the expressions of intent known as 'Aims' should represent the combined views of all the staff.

Aim 1 To inspire vigorous physical activity to promote normal healthy growth and physical development. Physical Education is most valuable when pupils' participation is enthusiastic, vigorous and wholehearted. All subsequent aims for a good programme depend on achieving this first aim.

Aim 2 To teach physical skills to develop skilful, well-controlled, versatile movement. We want pupils to enjoy moving well, safely and confidently. Physical Education makes a unique contribution to a child's physical development because the activities are experienced at first hand by doing them.

Aim 3 To help pupils become good learners as well as good movers. Knowledge, understanding and learning are achieved through a combination of doing, feeling and experiencing physical activity. Pupils are challenged to think for themselves, making decisions about their actions.

Aim 4 To develop pupils' self-confidence and self-esteem by appreciating the importance of physical achievement; by helping them to achieve; and by recognising and sharing such achievement with others.

Aim 5 To develop desirable social qualities, helping pupils get on well with one another by bringing them together in mutual endeavours. Friendly, co-operative, close relationships are an ever-present feature of Physical Education lessons.

Aim 6 To provide opportunities for exciting, almost adventurous actions (particularly climbing, swinging, balancing, jumping and landing) and vigorous exercise – seldom experienced away from school. We want our pupils to use these lessons as outlets for their energy and we want them to believe that exercise is good for you and your heart, and makes you feel and look better. We aim to encourage participation in a healthy lifestyle, long after pupils have left school.

The Gymnastic Activities Lesson Plan for Juniors – 30–35 minutes

One answer to the question 'What do we teach in a gymnastic activities lesson?' might be – 'All the natural actions and ways of moving of which the body is capable and which, if practised wholeheartedly and safely, ensure normal, healthy growth and physical development.'

It has been said that 'What you don't use, you lose.' Most pupils hardly ever use their natural capacity for vigorous running; jumping and landing from a height; rolling in a different direction; balancing on a variety of body parts; upending to take their weight on their hands; gripping, climbing and swinging on a rope; hanging, swinging or circling on a bar; or whole body bending, stretching, arching and twisting.

These natural movements and actions should be present in every gymnastic activities lesson, ensuring that pupils do not lose the ability to do them and have their physical development diminished.

A teacher's determination to inspire the class to use and not lose their natural physicality can be strengthened by observing how many children are collected in cars at the school gates. They are then transported home to their after school, house-bound, sedentary home lives.

Floorwork (12–15 minutes) starts the lesson and includes:
○ Activities for the legs, exploring and developing the many actions possible when travelling on feet, and ways to jump and land.

○ Activities for the body, including the many ways to bend, stretch, rock, roll, arch, twist, curl, turn, and the ways in which body parts receive, support and transfer the body weight in travelling and balancing.

○ Activities for the arms and shoulders, the least used parts of our body. We strengthen them by using them to hold all or part of the body weight on the spot or moving. This strength is needed in gripping, climbing, hanging, swinging and circling, and in levering on to and across apparatus, supported by the hands alone.

Apparatus Work (16–18 minutes) is the climax of the lesson, making varied, unique and challenging physical demands on pupils whose whole body – legs, arms and shoulders, back and abdominal muscles – has to work hard because of the more difficult tasks:

○ travelling on hands and feet, over, under, across and around obstacles, as well as vertically, often supported only on hands

○ jumping and landing from greater heights

○ rolling on to, along, from and across apparatus

○ balancing on high or narrow surfaces

○ upending to take all body weight on hands on apparatus above floor level

○ gripping, swinging, climbing and circling on ropes and bars.

Final Floor Activity (2 minutes) after the apparatus has been returned to its starting places around the sides, ends and corners of the hall, brings the whole class together again in a simple activity based on the lesson's main emphasis or theme. After the bustle of apparatus removal – the swishing of ropes along trackways, the creaking of climbing frames being wheeled away, the bumping of benches, planks, boxes and trestles – there is a quiet, calm, thoughtful and focused ending.

Three Ways to Teach Apparatus Work

1   **(Easiest Method) Pupils use all the apparatus freely, as they respond to tasks that relate to the lesson theme**. Several challenges provide non-stop apparatus work for infants and juniors. Pupils are stationary only when watching a demonstration, having a teaching point emphasised, or when being given the next task. This method is normally used with infant classes, because they are able to visit and use all pieces of apparatus, including their favourites – ropes and climbing frames.

    'Show me a still balance and beautifully stretched body shape on each piece of apparatus.' (Body shape awareness and balance)

    'Show me how you can approach each piece of apparatus going forward and leave going sideways.' (Space awareness – directions)

    'Leader, show your partner one touch only on each piece of apparatus, then off to the next piece.' (Partner work)

2   **Groups stay and work at one set of apparatus**. Repetition helps pupils improve and remember a series of linked actions. The task is the same for all groups, based on the lesson theme.

    'Make your hands important in arriving on, and your feet important in leaving the apparatus.' (Body parts awareness)

    'Can you include swings on to and off apparatus; a swing into a roll; and a swing to take all the weight on your hands?' (Swinging)

    'Travel from opposite sides, up to, on, along and from the apparatus, to finish in your partner's starting place.' (Partner work)

    Groups rotate to the next apparatus after about five minutes and will work at three sets in a lesson, rotating clockwise one lesson, and anti-clockwise the next, to meet all apparatus every two lessons.

3   **Each group practises a different, specific skill on each piece of apparatus - balancing, rolling, climbing, for example**. This method of teaching is more difficult than the other two because it needs more technical knowledge, and because the teacher is giving five or six sets of instructions instead of one. As it is a direct challenge to 'skills hungry' pupils, it is very popular.

    Benches 'At upturned benches, slowly balance and walk forward. Look straight ahead. Feel for the bench before you step on it.'

    Ropes 'Grip strongly with hands together and feet crossed. Can you take one hand off, while swinging, to prove a good foot grip?'

    Low cross box 'A face vault is like a high bunny jump to cross the box, as you twist over, facing the box top all the way.'

    Climbing frames 'Travel by moving hands only, then feet only.'

    Mats 'Roll sideways with body curled small and then with body long and stretched' (log roll).

    Groups rotate to the next piece of apparatus after about five minutes, rotating clockwise one lesson, and anti-clockwise the next lesson, meeting all apparatus every two lessons.

Organising Groups For Junior School Apparatus Work

Groups of five or six pupils are appropriate for junior school apparatus work, and pupils are placed in their mixed groups in the first lesson in September. Pupils are told 'These are your groups and starting places for apparatus work.' For the four or five sessions' development of a lesson, the same groups go to the same starting places, becoming more expert in lifting, carrying and placing their apparatus in that position.

From their regular starting positions, groups rotate clockwise, probably with time to work at three different sets of apparatus. At the end of the apparatus work, groups return to their own apparatus to move it back to the sides and ends of the room from which it was originally carried. The floor is now clear for the incoming class. In the next lesson, the groups will move anti-clockwise to work at the other three sets of apparatus.

This recommended system for ensuring that apparatus can be lifted, carried and placed in position quickly and easily, needs the co-operation of all the teachers. Before the lessons start in the morning or afternoon, the portable apparatus is placed around the sides and ends of the hall adjacent to where it will be used. Each group will only have to carry it 2–3 metres. A well-trained class can have the apparatus in place in 30 seconds. After all lessons are finished each day, as much of the apparatus as possible should remain in the hall, in corners, against or on the platform, or at the sides and ends of the room. Mats can be stored vertically behind frames, benches and boxes.

Positioning of Apparatus During Lessons

The teacher needs to provide varied actions and different physical demands as pupils progress from apparatus to apparatus to meet a challenging, interesting series of tasks which include:

a climbing and swinging on ropes

b rolling on mats, from benches, along low box

c balancing on inverted benches, planks, along low box

d running and jumping on to mats, across, along and from benches

e climbing on climbing frames

f taking weight on hands on mats, benches, planks, low boxes

g jumping and landing from a height from a bench or box

h circling or hanging from metal pole between trestles

i lying and pulling along a bench or down an inclined plank.

A safe environment is ensured by providing:

a mats where pupils are expected to land from a height

b mats that are well away from walls, windows, doors or other obstacles such as a piano, trolleys or chairs, and well away from the landing areas of adjacent apparatus

c height and width of apparatus that are appropriate for the age of the class – not too narrow to balance on, and not too high to jump from.

Mats are used to cushion a landing from a height and to roll on. We do not need mats under ropes or around climbing frames because we do not ask pupils to jump down from a height. If mats are placed around climbing frames, pupils often behave in a foolhardy way, enticed into dangerous jumping.

Fixed and portable apparatus

In the lesson plans that follow, the equipment continually being referred to and shown in the apparatus layouts includes the following items:

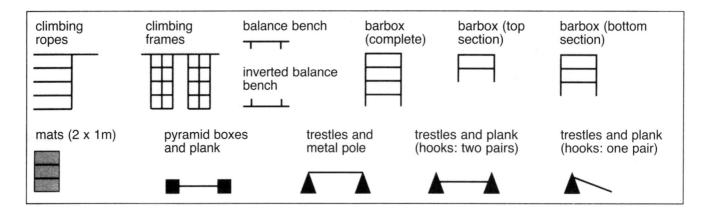

Minimum number recommended:

- ○ 12 mats 2 × 1 m

- ○ 3 balance benches

- ○ 1 barbox that can be divided into two smaller boxes by lifting off the top section; the remaining lower section should have a platform top fitted

- ○ 1 pair pyramid boxes and one plank

- ○ 1 × pair of 0.9 m, 1 m, and 1.4 m trestles

- ○ 1 metal pole to join pairs of trestles

- ○ 2 planks with two pairs of hooks

- ○ 2 planks with one pair of hooks

A Pattern for Teaching and Improving a Gymnastic Activities Action

Using 'Travelling' as an example

1   **Quickly into action**. With few words, clearly explain the task and challenge the class to start. For example 'Can you plan to travel, using your feet, sometimes going forwards, and sometimes in another direction?'

2   **While class is working**. Emphasise the main points, one at a time. There is no need to stop a well-behaved class who are working quietly every time you need to make a teaching point. 'Find quiet spaces in all parts of the room – the sides, ends, corners, as well as the middle.' 'Work so quietly that I can't hear you.' 'Travel on straight lines, never curving round, following someone.' 'Look over your shoulder if going backwards.'

3   **Identify and praise good work while class is working**. The teacher needs to circulate round the outside of the room, looking in to see as much of the work as possible. 'Well done, Thomas. I liked your skipping forwards and bouncing sideways.' 'Nathalie, your hopscotch is a great idea.' 'Sarah, your slow, careful running backwards with high knees lifting, is a neat, safe way to travel.'

4   **Demonstrations accompanied by teacher comment are the quickest way to increase the class repertoire**. It saves time if the demonstrators have been told what aspect of movement they are about to be asked to demonstrate. 'We will be looking at your beautifully stretched body in your jumps, and the soft, quiet way you let your knees and ankles give when you land.' 'Stop and watch Daniel's lively, quiet bouncing with feet parting and closing, going sideways. And look at Charlotte's galloping backwards with a strong arm swing.'
    Beware of stopping the class too often to use a demonstration. Make these stoppages brief, between 12 and 15 seconds.

5   **Further practice should follow a demonstration with reminders of the good things seen**. Pupils enjoy copying something they never thought of trying – particularly when it has been warmly praised and approved of. 'Thank you for those excellent demonstrations. Practise again, and try to improve your travelling by using something of what you have just seen. Use your whole body strongly, but quietly. Your feet can travel together or apart, or one after the other.'

6   **Demonstrations (by an individual, a small group or half of the class) with follow-up comments by the pupils are used to let pupils reflect on and evaluate their own and others' performances**. Such comments and judgements guide the next stage of planning for improvement. 'Watch this group of four working and tell me which travelling actions you like best, and say which directions you saw being used.' This is followed by a brief look at the pupils mentioned.

7   **Demonstrators and those making comments are thanked and more class practice lets them try some of the good things seen**. Beware of using demonstrations with follow-up comments more than once or twice in the lesson because they are time-consuming.

Progressing Gymnastic Activities over the 4 or 5 weeks of the Lesson's Development

Using 'Stepping' as an example of an activity to be developed

Lessons 1 and 2

a   Concentrate on the **'What?'**, the actions, their correct form, and how the body parts concerned are working.

  'Can you step quietly and neatly, visiting all parts of the room? Travel on straight lines, never following anyone.'

  'Which parts of the foot can support you? Tip toes, insides or outsides? Long or short steps or a mixture?'

  'Can you vary the idea of stepping, not always passing your feet?' (Chasse, crossover, toes down and swing.)

b   Insist on good, clear body shapes to make everything look better and be more demanding.

  'Step out nice and tall as you travel. Can you show me your clear arms, legs and body shape? Are you long and stretched or is there a body shape change somewhere?'

Lessons 2 and 3

Concentrate on the **'Where?'** of the movement, adding variety and quality by good use of own and whole floor space, directions and levels.

'Can you sometimes step on the spot, (particularly when you are in a crowded area) and sometimes use the whole room space – sides, corners, ends as well as middle.'

'Stepping actions sideways and backwards can be interesting – sliding, stepping-closing (chasse) or cross-stepping over, as well as feet passing normally. The leading leg can swing in many directions.'

Lessons 3 and 4

Consider the **'How?'** of the movements and the way that changes of speed and effort (force) might make the work look more controlled and neat, as well as giving them greater variety, contrast and interest.

'Within your stepping, can you include a change of speed? It might be slow, slow; quick, quick, 3, 4; slow, slow. Flat, flat; tip toes, tip toes, 3, 4; flat, flat.. This is interesting if a change of direction accompanies the speed change. Side, slow, slow; forward, quick, quick, 3, 4; side, slow, slow.' 'Can you make parts of your travelling small, soft, quiet, and make parts bigger, firmer, stronger?' (On the spot, keep it soft, 1, 2, 3, 4; on the move, big strong strides, 1, 2, 3, 4.)

Lessons 4 or Lessons 4 and 5

Ask for **sequences** that draw together all the practising, learning, adapting and remembering that have taken place during the previous lessons and aim for almost non-stop action, working harder for longer with enthusiasm, understanding and concentration.

'In your 3 or 4 part sequence, can you include: varied stepping actions, interesting use of space, and a change of speed or force somewhere?'

The Use of Themes in Teaching Gymnastic Activities

Week after week, month after month, the teacher and class come into the school hall and see the same apparatus, apparently offering the same limited set of activities every time. In dance, we continually move on to learning and performing new dances and building a huge repertoire. In games, the new seasons bring their different sports and the varied games implements provide an interesting and exciting range – including new games created by the teacher and pupils.

Gymnastic activities lessons are made different through applying a new idea, emphasis or theme each month. We do not simply 'do' the basic action. We do it, focusing on a particular aspect of movement, to improve in understanding and versatility, as well as in competence. A theme is a particular aspect of movement chosen by the teacher as a focal point around which to build a series of lessons.

At the very beginning of the series of four or five lessons during which an individual lesson is repeated, it is recommended that the pupils are 'put in the picture' regarding their lesson's main aims or emphases. In cases where they are going to be assessed on the outcome of the lesson, it is essential to explain to them what new skills, knowledge and understanding they will be expected to demonstrate. Identifying the lesson theme or main emphasis to the class is also a way for the teacher to put him or herself 'in the picture' about the main objectives of the lesson and to focus on them.

Start of year themes with a new class, will have an emphasis on good behaviour; sensible, safe sharing of floor and apparatus space; immediate responses to commands and challenges set by the teacher; establishing a tradition of wholehearted, vigorous effort and a co-operative attitude towards one's classmates; and co-operating with others to lift, carry and place apparatus quietly, sensibly and safely.

A suggested set of six progressive themes for a month to month programme

1 **Body parts awareness** for better controlled, safer, more correct activity. 'Show me varied ways to travel, using one foot, both feet, or one foot after the other.'

2 **Body shape awareness** for improved poise, better posture and firmer body tension. 'Can you run and jump up high with feet together and long, straight legs?'

3 **Space awareness** for improved variety, quality and interest, and safer practising. 'Can you travel all round the room, using feet only, sometimes going forwards, and sometimes sideways?'

4 **Effort awareness** for more interesting contrasts, better quality and stronger work. 'As you travel in a variety of ways can you include actions that are small, light and gentle, and actions that are large, lively and strong?'

5 **Sequences** for longer, harder, versatile work, stamping it with own personality. 'Make up a sequence you can remember, of three or four joined-up actions and changing body shapes on different body parts.' (Standing, kneeling, lying, sitting, upended on shoulders, arched on back or front.)

6 **Partner work** for new, enjoyable, sociable, more demanding experiences not possible on one's own, and to extend movement understanding because you need to recognise partner's actions. 'Stand, facing each other. Can you, with a little bend of knees as a start signal, bounce at the same speed? Can you do opposites, with one going up as the other comes down?'

A Progressive Series of Themes for a Gymnastic Activities Programme

An example from parts of lessons based on 'ways to travel'

Floorwork	Apparatus Work

Theme 1. Body parts awareness – for neater, better controlled, safer, more correct activity.

Floorwork

a Show me varied ways to travel, using one foot, both feet, or one foot after the other. As you travel about, slowly, using hands and feet, can you make different parts of your body go first?

Apparatus Work

a Plan to visit many pieces of apparatus. 'Feel' the different ways your hands and feet can:
   1 support you (for example, as you hang, swing, crawl, circle, roll, slide, skip, jump, balance.)
   2 go from apparatus to apparatus, putting hands on the apparatus, and show me a bunny jump with straight arms and well bent legs.

Theme 2. Body shape awareness – for improved poise, better posture and firmer body tension.

Floorwork

a Can you run and jump up high with feet together and long, straight legs?
b Can you run and jump up high to show me a wide shape like a star?

Apparatus Work

a Run quietly round the room, not touching any apparatus. When I call 'Stop!', show me a clear body shape on the nearest apparatus.
b Run round again and when I stop you next time, show me a different, firm body shape.

Theme 3. Space awareness – for improved variety, quality and interest, and safer practising.

Floorwork

a Can you travel all round the room, using feet only, sometimes forwards, and sometimes going sideways? Which are best for going forwards? Which are best for going sideways?

Apparatus Work

a Can you arrive on and leave the apparatus at different places and in different ways?
b Take weight on hands, with straight arms and bent legs. Bring feet down slowly in a new floor space.

Theme 4. Effort awareness – for more interesting contrasts, better quality, and stronger work.

Floorwork

As you travel in a variety of ways, can you include actions that are small, light and gentle, and actions that are large, lively and strong?

Apparatus Work

Travel freely. Show me strong, firm balances on apparatus that contrast with easier travelling actions in between. Can you do a vigorous upward jump, off, then a soft 'giving' landing.

Theme 5. Sequences – for longer, harder, versatile work, stamping it with own personality.

Floorwork

Work in a small floor space and show me two or more ways to travel on feet or feet and hands. Can you give each action a name? Show me a still start and finish.

Apparatus Work

Start in a still, nicely balanced position on the floor. Travel on to a piece of apparatus and show me a neat, still balance position.

Theme 6. Partner work – for new, more exciting experiences not possible on your own.

Floorwork

Follow your leader's varied travelling.

Apparatus Work

Follow on to and along each piece of apparatus.

National Curriculum Requirements for Gymnastic Activities – Key Stage 2: The Main Features

'The government believes that two hours of physical activity a week, including the National Curriculum for Physical Education and extra-curricular activities, should be an aspiration for all schools. This applies to all stages.'

Programme of study *Pupils should be taught to:*

a create and perform fluent sequences on the floor and using apparatus

b include variations in level, speed and directions in their sequences.

Attainment target *Pupils should be able to demonstrate that they can:*

a link skills, techniques and ideas and apply them appropriately, showing precision, control and fluency

b compare and comment on skills, techniques and ideas used in own and others' work and use this understanding to improve their own performances by modifying and refining skills and techniques.

Main NC headings when considering assessment, achievement and progression

○ **Planning** – in a focused, thoughtful, safe way, thinking ahead to an intended outcome. Evidence of satisfactory planning can be seen in:

  a good decision-making, sensible, safe judgements and good understanding of what was asked for

  b an understanding of the elements that enhance quality, variety and contrast in 'movement'

  c the expression of personal qualities such as optimism, enthusiasm, and a capacity for hard work in pursuit of improvement.

○ **Performing and improving performance** successfully is the main aim. In a satisfactory performance a pupil demonstrates:

  a well-controlled, neat and accurate work, concentrating on the main feature of the task

  b the ability to practise to improve skilfulness, performing safely

  c whole-hearted and vigorous activity, sharing the space sensibly and unselfishly, with a concern for own and others' safety

  d the ability to remember and repeat actions.

○ **Linking actions** – as pupils build longer, more complex sequences of linked actions in response to the stimuli, demonstrating that they are:

  a working harder for longer, showing a clear beginning, middle and end to their sequence

  b pursuing almost non-stop, vigorous and enjoyable action.

○ **Reflecting and evaluating** – as pupils describe what they and others have done, say what they liked about a performance, give an opinion on how it might be improved; and then make practical use of such reflection to plan again to improve.

Year 4 Gymnastic Activities Programme

Pupils should be able to:

Autumn	Spring	Summer
1 Co-operate sensibly to provide a safe, quiet working environment.	1 Consolidate particular skills by practice and repetition.	1 Use swinging as an aid to movement in floor and apparatus work.
2 Respond readily and quickly to instructions.	2 Develop body-shape awareness in held and moving positions.	2 Practise rolls, forwards, back, side to side, aided by impetus of the swing.
3 Respond whole-heartedly and with vigour to challenges.	3 Include clear shapes within sequences to enhance them and provide variety and contrast.	3 Swing up to handstand, choosing arm or leg swing as own preference.
4 Share space unselfishly to enable self and others to work properly and safely.	4 Learn safe, traditional skills – rolls, cartwheels, vaults and balances.	4 Plan apparatus sequences to start and finish on the floor, away from apparatus.
5 Plan ahead to visualise the intended outcome.	5 Revise correct, safe grips and handholds on apparatus, and hands, arms and head position when inverted on hands.	5 Include swings, rolls and taking weight on hands within apparatus sequences.
6 Plan to include varied actions performed neatly and quietly.	6 Improve quality and variety with space features such as different directions, levels and own and general space.	6 Apply speed and effort factors to make work look more controlled, varied, demanding, interesting.
7 Develop a tradition of continuous work, always aware of the need to share space with others.	7 With still start and finish, practise, adapt, improve and be able to repeat longer, more complex sequences.	7 Work harder for longer with better control.
8 Include contrasts of speed, shape, effort and use of space to enhance performances.	8 Extend balance possibilities on floor and apparatus, always aware of clear shapes and different levels.	8 Balance, feeling contrast between one, firm, held balance and the more relaxed transfer to the next.
9 Practise, repeat, adapt and try to improve.	9 Recognise and describe good features of a demonstration.	9 Apply strong effort to develop strength and suppleness, and to exercise the heart and the lungs.
10 Use the full range of movement possible in the joints concerned.	10 Give the impression of habitually sustaining and enjoying energetic activity.	10 Make quick decisions, e.g. in matching a partner.
11 Practise different ways to do basic actions – travel, jump, roll, swing, climb, balance and take weight on hands.		11 Remember and repeat work exactly to enable partner to learn it.
12 Feel and understand how body parts work to support, receive and transfer body weight.		12 Be aware of features to watch in a partner's demonstration – actions; body parts involved; shapes; directions; speed and effort.
13 Comment generously on the main features of a performance observed, and what was liked.		13 Encourage demonstrators with favourable, encouraging comments.

Year 4

Lesson Plan 1 • 30-35 minutes
September

At the start of the year the lesson's main emphases include: *(a) creating a safe, caring, quiet atmosphere where all co-operate sensibly and unselfishly, particularly in sharing space; (b) establishing a tradition of immediate responses to instructions; (c) establishing a tradition of lessons being filled with vigorous, whole-hearted, physical activity.*

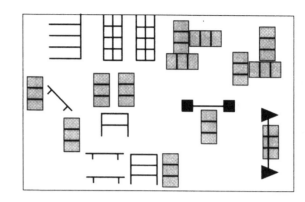

Floorwork
12—15 minutes

Legs

1 Show me your best running, keeping well away from others.

2 When I call 'Stop!' move quickly into your own space and show me a tall, stretched balance on tiptoes. Stop! (Repeat.)

3 Good running is quiet and you don't follow anyone. Visit all parts of the room and run on straight lines, not curves.

4 Lift heels, knees, arms and chest to make your running quiet and neat. Stop! (Well spaced, stretched on tiptoes.)

Body

1 Lie on your back, curled up tightly, with hands clasped under knees. Can you roll, slowly, from side to side?

2 Still curled up tightly, can you roll forwards and back on to shoulders and hands? Practise the strong hand push to stop the roll back and to start the roll forward.

Arms

1 Slowly, and keeping well away from others, show me ways that you can travel, using feet and hands.

2 Can you try movements using hands only, then feet only?

3 Can you vary your travelling by having front, back or side to the floor, or be upended, as in cartwheels?

Apparatus Work
16-18 minutes

1 Travel to all parts of the room, going in and out, along, across, and under apparatus, touching only mats and floor to start with.

2 When I call 'Stop!' quickly show me a fully stretched body on the nearest piece of apparatus. Stop! (Repeat.)

3 Travel up to, on and away from pieces of apparatus, using feet only. Use your feet well on floor and apparatus and show me how sensibly you are sharing space with others.

4 Travel on floor and apparatus, using feet and hands only.

5 Stay at your present group of apparatus to repeat, practise and improve the following.

   a Start and finish away from the apparatus in a floor space.

   b Include neat travelling on feet, and hands and feet.

   c Roll on mats, on apparatus or from apparatus.

   d At some point, which could be the very beginning or end, show me a beautifully stretched, still body.

Final Floor Activity
2 minutes

Start in a tall, still starting position. Run quietly and well, to visit all parts of the room, the sides, corners, ends and the middle. Run on straight lines and do not follow anyone.

Teaching notes and NC guidance
Development over 4 lessons

NC elements being emphasised:

a Being taught to be physically active.
b Responding readily to instructions.
c Planning, performing and reflecting among NC elements being emphasised.

Floorwork

Legs

1 Discourage any tendency towards anti-clockwise running, all following one another in a big circle, common in primary schools.

2 'Stop!' is an exercise in 'responding readily to instructions', an essential tradition, to be established every September.

3 Demonstrate with those who move along straight lines, looking out for and keeping well away from others.

4 Demonstrate with and praise those whose running appears to be lifting up off the floor, as they travel so lightly.

Body

1 The rocking starts with a swing to one side with hands and knees. Chin is on chest, keeping back rounded and easy to roll on.

2 For the roll back and forwards, hands are placed beside shoulders with thumb in and small finger out, with elbows lifted high. Going back is like the start of a backward roll. Going forwards, helped by the strong hands push, is like the end of a forward roll.

Arms

1 Insist on slow, thoughtful actions, not quick, untidy scampering.

2 Hands only, then feet only adventurous hand-walking and cartwheels, or an easy crawling action, walking forwards on hands as far as you can go, then walking feet up beside hands again.

3 Challenge them to vary the leading body parts (not always the head) and not always to have front towards floor.

Apparatus Work

1 This is an exercise in travelling on the floor, in a variety of ways, between apparatus. During apparatus work, the floor travelling is often ignored in favour of that on apparatus.

2 'Stop!' demands an instant response on the nearest piece of apparatus, and requires them to listen, while they are travelling. Praise those whose stretched body is on a part other than the easy feet or feet and hands.

3 Pursue vigour and whole-hearted, non-stop activity. Use eyes to see a space. Wait your turn in coming from apparatus on to the mats. Because it is feet only travelling, the ropes and frames are not included yet. Look out for and identify walking, running, jumping, bouncing, skipping, balancing, springing, hopscotching.

4 Much commenting by the circulating teacher, praising the wide variety of responses seen, helps expand the class repertoire.

5 *Plan* your travelling, rolling and balance. *Perform* it after much repetition, improving and remembering. *Reflect* after each performance, then adapt as necessary to bring about improvement.

Final Floor Activity

If they pretend to have chalk on their feet, they should leave their mark in corners, sides, ends.

Lesson Plan 2 ● 30-35 minutes
October

Emphasis on: *developing a tradition of quiet, continuous work with an awareness of the need for good spacing. The equally desirable tradition of whole-hearted participation means working the body strongly and using the full range of movement possible in the joints concerned.*

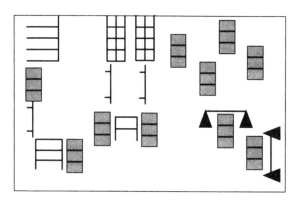

Floorwork
12—15 minutes

Legs

1 Join together a short walk, a short run and a vigorous high jump. Land quietly, using your arms to balance you, and be still. Look for a space and continue.

2 In your high jump, stretch every part of your body, with arms reaching up and toes and ankles stretched down.

3 Think of making a 'squashy' landing with knees giving to make a soft, quiet action.

Body

Balancing means that your body is on some small or unusual part or parts and wanting to 'wobble'.

1 Show me an easy balance on one foot. Stretch strongly the leg and arms not being used to make your body work hard.

2 Move to some other part or parts and show me a new balance. Once again, stretch hard the parts not being used.

3 Keep working at three or four different balances. Each time hold the position strongly. The stretching of non-supporting parts makes you work really hard and makes your balance position look more attractive and 'gymnastic'.

Arms

1 Keep your body in the crouched 'bunny jump' position with bent legs and straight arms. Keep your fingers spread with hands pointing forwards and travel in and out of the others.

2 Can you lift your 'bunny jump' high enough to place your shoulders over your hips over your hands?

Apparatus Work
16—18 minutes

1 Travel to different pieces of apparatus and find ways to move on them. Can you leave with a high jump and soft landing?

2 Start and finish away from each piece of apparatus. Show me your ways of travelling on floor and apparatus. Include movements using legs, arms, and can you show me a still, stretched balance?

3 Go from apparatus to apparatus, showing me a 'bunny jump' action on each with straight arms and bent legs.

4 Stay at your present piece of apparatus in small groups of about five to practise, repeat and improve the following.

    a Start and finish away from the apparatus.
    b Show varied ways of travelling up to it using legs.
    c Make your hands important in travelling on the apparatus, trying at some point to take all the weight on your hands.
    d At some point hold a beautifully still, stretched balance.

Final Floor Activity
2 minutes

Walking, running and long jumping, travel to all parts of the room.

Teaching notes and NC guidance
Development over 4 lessons

NC elements being emphasised:

a Exploring different means of jumping, balancing and taking weight on hands.
b Improving and repeating longer and increasingly complex sequences of movement.

Floorwork

Legs

1 A 3–4 metre line is long enough to include all three actions. The strength felt in the vigorous spring upwards should also be felt in the stretched body in its flight.

2 A full, clear body shape contributes to the appearance and the 'correctness' in a performance, and proves we are working hard.

3 Absorbing impact by a 'giving' in the knees and ankles becomes even more important from apparatus.

Body

1 In balancing, encourage them to stretch the body parts not supporting the body, to work harder and look better. No sagging!

2 Moving to an adjacent body part for support requires careful rolling, sitting, rocking, lowering, twisting, arching, levering.

3 Demonstrations by groups of good performers will help to swell the class repertoire in this difficult activity. Some might even work hard to hold a still handstand for two or three seconds.

Arms

1 The bunny jump travelling can be made more interesting by a twisting, zig zag pathway, side to side, over a line.

2 Two or three preliminary bounces on the hands can be done. 'Bounce, bounce, bounce and spring up!'

Apparatus Work

1 Teacher's commentary on the many actions being seen helps to spread ideas – climbing, swinging, rolling, sliding, pulling, vaulting, circling, hanging, balancing. Praise should be given for good high jumps up to and from apparatus.

2 Remember that hands and feet can support you on the floor in addition to the feet only, more commonly seen. The still, stretched balance could be the start or finish position, on toes away from the apparatus, or a held position on the apparatus.

3 Class can be asked to 'Show me your hands', hands held towards teacher to show straight arms with fingers pointing forwards. This strong, safe hand and arm position is now used. Going from apparatus to apparatus, with a high spring up to a bunny jump.

4 *Plan* for variety in leg travelling; varied uses and grips by hands; all weight on hands, carefully; and a whole body, stretched balance at some point – start, middle or finish. *Reflect*, then think about and *plan* how to alter it to improve it. *Perform* even better work.

Final Floor Activity

Short walk, short run, jump, with the jump the main part to be demonstrated, using all parts of the room.

Lesson Plan 3 • 30-35 minutes
November

Emphasis on: *developing quality and variety in the many natural body activities that children experience in a lively, varied, gymnastics lesson. As the term implies, 'natural body activities' includes all forms of travelling, jumping, landing, rolling, swinging, climbing, balancing and hanging.*

Floorwork
12–15 minutes

Legs

1 As you travel to all parts of the room, using legs only, can you include two or three different actions, performed quietly, neatly, and with an obvious contrast somewhere (e.g. quiet tiptoe walking; easy skipping with a full arm swing; and a vigorous upward jump)?

2 Remember that your travelling actions are good when they are neat, quiet and not following anyone. Travel on straight lines which means that you have to keep changing direction, not on a curve where everyone is following everyone.

Body

1 Experiment with different actions you can do while you travel on a variety of body parts.

2 If you start off, *balanced*, say, on one foot or one foot and one hand, can you *lower* to a larger body part such as shoulders or seat; then can you roll on to, for example, knees and elbows; then *swing up* to start all over again?

Arms

1 Show me some of the ways that you can plan to go from feet only, to being on hands only, to returning to feet only.

2 On the spot can you include handstands and bunny jumps? Low travels can be springs from low crouch on to hands; high travels can include cartwheels and handwalking.

Apparatus Work
16-18 minutes

1 Travel to all parts of the room, touching floor and mats only. Make your actions fit the spaces and the obstacles that you meet, using legs only (e.g. walk, run or skip on open floor; roll or leap across mats; spring or cartwheel over benches; step through spaces in frames; bounce, feet astride, along benches).

2 Now change to travelling on apparatus and floor and, once again let your many actions fit the places where you are travelling (e.g. swing on a rope; spring off a bench; cartwheel or roll across a mat; vault over a box or bench; balance on a bench; hang on a bar or rope; circle on a rope or bar).

3 Stay at your present group of apparatus in small groups to practise, repeat and improve the following.

  a Start and finish, in own floor space in a still, 'firm' position.

  b Plan to include a variety of natural actions to take you up to, on, along and away from the apparatus. Make these actions fit the places and the spaces where you are working.

  c Can you include some travelling on feet only; on different body parts; and on hands and feet, as we practised in our floorwork?

Final Floor Activity
2 minutes

Using feet only, travel to every part of the room using movements where your feet stay near to the floor as they travel.

Teaching notes and NC guidance
Development over 4 lessons

NC elements being emphasised:

a Making appropriate decisions quickly and planning their responses.

b Making judgements of performances and suggesting ways to improve.

Floorwork

Legs

1 'Contrast' comes from changes of effort (e.g. vigorous or gentle actions, firm or relaxed body) and speed used (slow, normal, accelerating or quick). The 'How?'

2 Thinking about the 'Where?', the straight line travelling is asked for to counter any tendency to the anti-clockwise travel in a big circle, common in primary schools, with all following all.

Body

1 Travelling on a variety of body parts, ideally, will include at least three examples as a good challenge. For example, a run into a jump, land, lower on to back, roll sideways right over on to front, stand and then cartwheel.

2 The example given can be offered to those who are less 'creative' to get them started quickly, and to give them something to develop and adapt as their own.

Arms

1 Emphasise 'Feet only on to hands only', not feet and hands. It sometimes helps to pretend that you are working on to, across or along a bench from a starting position on the floor.

2 Once again, direct teaching as in the previous, body activity, can give them all a varied sequence to practise, and then develop in their own way.

Apparatus Work

1 Quick reactions ('making appropriate decisions quickly') are needed to fit the actions to the small, large, wide or narrow spaces encountered.

2 Similar fitting of actions to spaces, but this time on floor and on apparatus. Plan to include actions that use hands, hands and feet, feet, and other large body parts for variety. Plan to use just the right amount of effort for a controlled, quality performance.

3 A sequence of natural actions, staying at a group of apparatus with four or five others only, to enable you to practise, repeat, remember and improve. *Plan* for variety and quality with a definite beginning, middle and end. *Perform* whole-heartedly to improve. *Reflect* and *evaluate*, adapt, practise, improve and remember.

Final Floor Activity

Walking, low skipping, running 'skimming' the floor, slipping sideways (low chasse).

Lesson Plan 4 • 30–35 minutes
December

Theme: *Body parts awareness and learning to 'feel' and understand how the body works and moves in its many ways to support, receive and transfer body weight.*

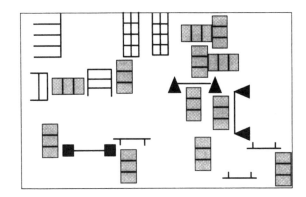

Floorwork
12–15 minutes

Legs

1   Practise soft, quiet upward jumps on the spot. Really stretch the ankles at take-off, and let them 'give' on landing. Feel the firm stretch in your whole body going up. Feel the gentle 'give' in ankles and knees on landing.

2   Skip around the room using the same good stretch in the pushing ankle. Let the opposite leg bend high forwards with its ankle well stretched and the opposite arm reach forwards as a balance. (Opposite arm and thigh horizontal.)

Body

Stand with feet apart. Slowly bend down leading with your head. Neck joints, shoulders, back, waist, hips, knees and ankles all 'give' until you are crouched on two feet. Now rise up in the opposite order, stretching ankles, knees, hips, waist, back, shoulders, neck and finish by stretching arms high above head. Lower arms and repeat, feeling the exact order in which the joints close and open.

Arms

Travel slowly on hands and feet, in and out of the others. Try keeping arms and legs straight, together or apart for a very strong movement. You can move arms only, then legs only; or left side, then right side; or opposite as in crawling. A really strong action is bouncing along, springing everything up off the floor.

Apparatus Work
16–18 minutes

1   Walk, run, jump or skip around all the apparatus, touching only the floor and the mats. When I call 'Stop!' quickly find a place on the nearest piece of apparatus, with both feet off the apparatus and ankles stretched strongly. Stop! (Repeat.)

2   When I stop you next time, show me a fully stretched body on a piece of apparatus. Stop! Now, slowly curl into a rounded shape.

3   Next time, can you be stretched on a different body part on a different piece of apparatus? Stop! Slowly curl everything in.

4   Walk to many pieces of apparatus and try out the ways your hands can lift, lever, jump, circle, twist you on to apparatus.

5   Stay at your present set of apparatus, in small groups of five or six to work hard at the following activities to feel how our different body parts work to receive, support and transfer our weight on, across, under, around, along and from the varied apparatus.
   Mats – rolling
   Climbing frames – climbing
   Ropes – swinging or climbing
   Trestles, poles, planks – travelling
   Inverted benches, trestle – balancing
   Boxes, mats, bench – running and jumping; rolling; weight on hands

Final Floor Activity
2 minutes

Can you make different parts of your body lead in your travelling (knees, head, elbow, etc.)?

Teaching notes and NC guidance
Development over 4 lessons

NC elements being emphasised:

a Developing skills by exploring and making up activities and by expressing themselves imaginatively.

b Sustaining energetic activity and showing an understanding of what happens to the body during exercise.

Floorwork

Legs

1 The ankle joint is seldom fully stretched in everyday life and is often stiff and weak. Demonstrate with strong, supple pupils to show the strong downward stretch and drive at take-off, and the soft, controlled, 'give' in ankles on landing.

2 The stretch in both the take-off ankle and the one high ahead on leading leg is looked for here. The one driving foot and ankle have to work hard to propel the whole body weight, and the one receiving foot and ankle work hard to receive and support all the body weight.

Body

Teacher can talk them down, joint by joint. Class can talk through the opposite actions. 'Unroll ankles, knees, hips, waist, lower, middle, upper back, neck, shoulders, elbows, wrists to full stretch.'

Arms

By travelling slowly and using body parts to their fullest movement, we are able to recognise the actions, and we are working our bodies strongly. Quick scampering with most weight on feet is neither attractive to look at, or good exercise.

Apparatus Work

1 'Feet and ankles off apparatus' ensures an interesting position on a variety of other body parts. (Seat, front, back, side, shoulders.)

2 They have to plan a stopping position where they are fully stretched, and from which they are able to curl slowly.

3 Demonstrations at the previous activity should extend the range presented here.

4 They are thinking 'Hands' and trying to name the many actions possible in lifting us on to, across, around, along, under, up and down apparatus.

Mats
Feel chin on chest going forwards, shoulders contacting first (not head) and feel heels close to seat before standing.

Climbing frames
Thumbs under the bars, fingers on top for all climbing, for a strong, safe grip.

Ropes
Hands together for a strong grip for swinging or to start the climb as you lift both feet.

Inverted benches, trestle
Balance on small or unusual body parts, or small or unusual apparatus surfaces, without wobbling.

Trestles
Remain on for most of the time as you travel under, along, around, across with as many grips as possible.

Boxes, plank, bench
Excellent contrast in body actions – lively run and jump; smooth, easy rolls; and a moment's stillness on hands.

Final Floor Activity

Ask 'How many body parts can you lead with in the next two minutes? Count as you go.'

Lesson Plan 5 • 30-35 minutes
January

Theme: *Body shape awareness in held positions and on the move. Awareness of long, wide, curled or twisted body shapes within own performances and those of others. Shape's contribution to good style and to efficiency of movements.*

Floorwork
12—15 minutes

Legs

Stand tall and ready to go with all parts of your body stretched strongly. Run and jump with a long, then a wide, then a tucked body shape in flight. Let your knees 'give' for a quiet, soft landing, but keep your upper body straight for a good balanced finish. Stretched arms for balance can be forward, above head or sideways.

Body

Using different starting positions, can you change from one wide body shape to another (e.g. from standing, feet and arms stretched wide; to front support position on floor, spread wide; to side falling on one foot and one hand, body side on to floor with upper arm and leg stretched to make a wide shape; to back lying, stretched wide; to balanced on shoulders, feet wide, etc.)?

Arms

1   With hands on floor, can you jump your feet in the air, kicking them strongly and keeping them stretched (kicking horses)?

2   Practise 'bunny jumps' on two hands with legs kept curled.

Apparatus Work
16-18 minutes

1   As you travel all around the room on floor and mats only, can you emphasise your body shape? For example, very straight or well bent arms and legs in your walking or running; or bounding along on two feet, wide or lifting into a tuck.

2   When I call 'Stop!' quickly find a place on the nearest apparatus where you can balance, hang or support yourself and show me a clear body shape. Stop! (Repeat.)

3   Travel, using all apparatus and find a variety of places on, under, around, across, hanging where you can show me a variety of body shapes which make your held position look neat and which are quite difficult to hold.

4   In your small groups of five or six, start at your present set of apparatus to repeat, improve and be able to demonstrate the following:

   a   Start away from apparatus; travel up to, on and away from the apparatus to finish in your own floor space, and include...

   b   Travelling through contrasting shapes (e.g. rolls contrasting with stretched and wide jumps; rolling into a wide balance; twisting on and stretching along, etc.). Remember to include poised and still starting and finishing positions which do not always have to be on feet.

Final Floor Activity
2 minutes

Show me a triangle of three jumps to bring you back to your starting place. Include three different shapes in the air.

Gymnastic Activities

Teaching notes and NC guidance
Development over 4 lessons

NC elements being emphasised:

a   Emphasising changes of shape through gymnastic actions.
b   Adopting good posture and the appropriate use of the body.

Floorwork

Legs

Use a short, 3–4-metre run only, since the jump is the main activity. Performing on a triangle helps to provide a repeating start and finish place. Body shape interest is widespread – erect body at start, three whole body shapes in flight, and good use of stretched arms for balance in flight and on landing.

Body

To help them into action in this difficult challenge, a series of three or four positions with their linking actions can be suggested and/or led by the teacher. During the following weeks they will adapt and develop their own series.

Arms

1   Arms and legs are strongly stretched in the kicking horses. Straight arms are strong and do not tend to give as slightly bent arms do. The kicking action, front to rear, seems to assist and keep putting the body into balance.

2   Bent legs are short levers and bounce up into the bunny jump position more easily and quickly than straighter legs. Two or three preliminary little bounces of feet up and off floor, are a help as you gather for the strong bounce up and on to hands. They aim to place hips above shoulders above hands, all in a line.

Apparatus Work

1   No action can be done without a body shape. Be aware of the shape and work hard to make it full and firm. Remember that it always looks better, and is more efficient and correct when the shape is right.

2   Stop and respond immediately, to show a clear, whole body shape on the nearest piece of apparatus. If there is a body part not touching the apparatus or supporting you, stretch it firmly away, to enhance the appearance of the performance.

3   More leisurely travelling now, to visit all apparatus in turn to show varied, still body shapes (e.g. stretched hanging from a bar of climbing frame; curled hanging from two ropes; curled around a metal pole; back arched on a mat; wide, side on to a climbing frame, holding with one hand and one foot).

4   *Plan*: (a) your pathway from start to finish (b) your choice of actions that highlight changing shape while travelling. *Perform* two or three times to improve. *Reflect*, adapt, repeat, improve, remember.

Final Floor Activity

Discourage long-sided triangles. A 3-metre side is sufficient because the jumps, not the runs, are the main parts. What shapes? What take-off and landing actions?

Lesson Plan 6 • 30-35 minutes
February

Theme: *Direct teaching of simple, safe Gymnastic Activities.*

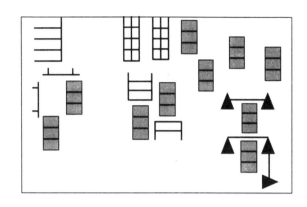

Floorwork
12—15 minutes

Legs

1   Skip jumping on the spot with good stretch in ankles at take-off, and a soft 'give' on landing. Do four to each side of room.

2   Three skip jumps on the spot and a tucked jump (knees high, lifted to chest) on four. Turn to face next wall and repeat.

3   Can you continue this activity and add your own jump on count of four, e.g. tuck, jacknife, star, twist with heels up and back to one side?

Body

1   Roll to face opposite way. Sit with feet wide apart and arms straight and down by sides. Lean over, straight to one side, on to back, with legs still wide and straight, pointing up. Now complete turn by swinging leg down to floor and pulling body up to a seated position again, legs still wide and straight.

2   Now, can you do it all the way back to where you began?

Arms

Cartwheels. An easy introduction is to ask class to pretend that they are standing on a big hoop, with feet apart. One hand reaches down on to another part of hoop, feet push off and second hand touches down further around the hoop, then feet return to hoop, one after the other, with twist of body.

Apparatus Work
16—18 minutes

Mats
Revise cartwheels. Try a backward roll from sitting, heel close to seat, hands up above shoulders, thumbs near to ears. Back is rounded and chin is on chest. Roll back on to flat hands on floor, thumbs still near ears.

Upturned benches and mats
Balance walk forwards. From balanced standing on bench, the leading foot feels its way alongside the supporting surface. The foot carefully feels for the balance surface before putting weight down.

Ropes
Try swinging with hands together and feet crossed on the rope. A strong foot grip means that you can take one hand away without sliding off rope.

Cross low boxes
Face vault is a bunny jump over the box. You approach at right angles, and place hands obliquely on box. With a two-footed take-off, spring up and over the box, seat well up and over hands, and knees bent. You face the box all the way across.

Climbing frames
Travel by moving the feet by themselves, then the hands by themselves. Can you do this in a rectangle of 4–6 spaces?

Trestles, pole, planks
Show me those parts of the apparatus where you can hang, using hands only, hands and feet, hands and one leg, tummy, backs of knees. Can you hang and stretch, hang and curl?

Final Floor Activity
2 minutes

Can you do four skip jumps on the spot, then do four little ones travelling forwards, then four to one side, then four straight back, then four to one side to finish where you started?

Teaching notes and NC guidance
Development over 4 lessons

NC elements being emphasised:

a Exploring different means of rolling, swinging, jumping and taking weight on hands.

b Developing their skills by exploring and making up activities.

Floorwork

Legs

1 A full, strong stretching in the ankle joint at take-off, and a silent, soft 'give' in the ankles on landing, are the main features to start with.

2 Good height is needed to give you time to add the tucked position.

3 Look out for, praise and demonstrate with those whose big effort is producing sufficient height to do a clear, firm and impressive shape, followed by a beautifully quiet, controlled landing.

Body

1 Circle roll is a favourite way to change direction. For example, forward roll to straddle sitting. Circle roll back to face your starting position.

2 Class perform circle roll away from the teacher to face the opposite wall, then perform to come back to starting place again.

Arms

Cartwheels can be low and almost circular for learners, progressing to a straight line for more capable performers.

Apparatus Work

Mats

Cartwheel with greater comfort on a mat. 'Hand, push off to other hand, foot, foot.'

Upturned benches

Stand astride bench. Mount to balance standing. Do not look down. Feel your way along balance surface, keeping contact with some part of both feet. The walking forwards can be enhanced by a high knee raising of non-supporting leg. You can also balance walk backwards and sideways.

Ropes

Hands together means hands are both working strongly during swings. On a climb, reach up with one hand, then other hand, then first hand next to second hand for the hands together pull.

Cross low boxes

High bunny jumps become face vaults across box. Legs are kept bent, arms are straight and you twist around and off, facing box all the time.

Climbing frames

There will be much stretching and curling as you travel, hands only, feet only. When hand grip is used, stress 'Fingers grip over one side away from you, thumbs grip under and towards you.'

Trestles

A 'gripping' activity, full of variety which will deserve to be demonstrated to increase the class and the teacher's repertoire.

Final Floor Activity

A set of 20 jumps as a whole class activity, performed slowly and softly, is a pleasing ending.

Lesson Plan 7 • 30-35 minutes
March

Theme: *Space awareness and understanding the 'where' of movement as we share the floor and apparatus with others moving vigorously. The variety and quality of the work is improved by good and varied use of directions, levels and pathways and by understanding the difference between own space and general space.*

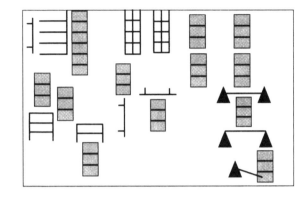

Floorwork
12—15 minutes

Legs

Travel using your legs and include different directions. Can you show me which actions travel easily in sideways or backward directions, and which most easily in a forward direction (e.g. chasse or slip step sideways, small skipping steps backwards)?

Body

With your body in a bridge-like shape, can you travel in different directions (e.g. forwards, backwards, sideways on hands and feet, with front, back or side towards the floor)?

Arms

Experiment with one, two or alternate hands supporting you. Can you take your legs up into the air space above your head then bring them down in a new space on the floor (e.g. low 'bunny jumps' across a line or high cartwheels along a line)?

Apparatus Work
16—18 minutes

1   Show me a lively leg activity in your own personal space. Then travel on floor and apparatus, occasionally changing direction, up to, on or from the apparatus to a new own space to start again.

2   Can you approach apparatus facing forwards and leave it facing sideways or, very carefully, backwards?

3   Stay at your own starting group places in fives or sixes to practise, improve and remember the following.

Mats
Can you plan and practise a sequence of three or four bridge-like shapes with the emphasis on changing levels?

Climbing frames
Can you travel, using a small group of 4–6 spaces, then travel using the whole frame? Plan to let different parts of your body lead.

Ropes, benches, mats
As you swing can you demonstrate direction changes? Your swing can start from mat, bench or after a short run and you can swing by jumping on to a swinging rope.

Trestles, poles, planks
All stay on the apparatus, sharing it sensibly as you travel along, across, around, or under, sometimes with your body very near or well away from the apparatus.

Long bench, mat, cross bench, mat
Zig-zag along the long bench and mat. At the return cross bench, show me a running high jump.

Boxes, mats
Arrive on the apparatus facing forwards. Leave facing another way.

Final Floor Activity
2 minutes

Run with four easy actions, then four with high knees in your own floor space. Then run normally all around the room and back to your own floor space.

Teaching notes and NC guidance
Development over 4 lessons

NC elements being emphasised:

a   Changes of direction and level to be emphasised through gymnastic actions.
b   Practising, adapting, improving and repeating longer and more complex sequences of movement.

Floorwork

Legs

Establish good use of space to practise and to avoid impeding others. Going backwards needs to be slow and careful, looking back over one shoulder. A triangular pathway uses space well (e.g. forwards, then sideways, then backwards to starting place).

Body

Very easy travel on feet with body arched forwards, back or to one side. Quite easy travel on hands and feet. Difficult travel, walking on hands with arch below knees.

Arms

One-handed twisting, low bunny jumps. Two-handed, high bunny jumps. Handstands. Alternate hands cartwheels.

Apparatus Work

1   Focus on 'My space and whole room space, and direction changes.'

2   While we want virtually non-stop activity, we should sometimes wait until there is plenty of space before leaving apparatus, sideways or backwards, for our own and others' safety.

Mats

'Bridging' can include sitting (bridge under knees); side falling on one hand and one foot; face down on hands and feet, or on knees and elbows; arched with back to floor on hands and feet, or on shoulders and feet; standing arched forwards, sideways or to rear.

Climbing frames

You can weave in and out of small groups of spaces with hands, head or feet leading. In using the whole frame, you can lead up with head, to side with one side, down with feet.

Ropes, bench, mats

Change direction in flight, on landing, after landing.

Trestles, poles, mats

Group activity with non-stop action, sharing apparatus and floor beneath. Try to plan pathway from floor start to floor finish. Include some under, on, around, across for variety.

Benches, mats

Zig-zag travel can be on one or both hands, side to side; feet together or alternate; both hands and feet, on to and from (e.g. bunny jumps, cat springs); starting beside or further away from bench; across without touching.

Boxes, mats

Much teacher commentary to accompany the actions on (roll, cat spring, jump, bunny jump, step, swing of leg or arm) and off (sideways or carefully backwards, stepping, jumping, rolling).

Final Floor Activity

A three part activity. Run into a space near you, taking four counts to arrive. Run on the spot with four sets of high knee liftings. Run, using a lot of room space, back to your own starting place to finish, standing still. Repeat.

Lesson Plan 8 ● 30-35 minutes
April

Theme: *Balance, and some of the ways in which the body can move into, hold and move from balanced stillness.*

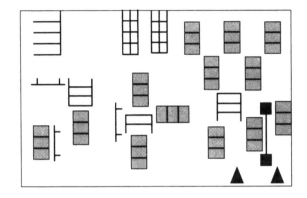

Floorwork
12—15 minutes

Legs

Stand, balanced and stretched tall, on tiptoes with arms and heels high, or even on one foot only. Use a short run into a good space, jump up high and land, beautifully balanced. Use stretched arms strongly to help control in the air, and on landing. Experiment with feet positions on landing to give you easy balance. (Jumping into balance.)

Body

Can you hold your body in balance on three different bases, and can you make the body shape different with each balance? See if rolls can help you to link your balances together. For example, star shape on one foot; lower and roll up into a long stretch on shoulders; roll back over one shoulder into a bridge on hands and tiptoes.

Arms

Teach elbow balance. From a crouch position with feet apart, place hands on floor, shoulder width apart and under shoulders. Bend elbows slightly to place them inside and under knees. Tilt body forwards slowly, from feet on to hands, until toes come a short distance off the floor, and you are balancing on hands only. (Tilting into balance.)

Apparatus Work
16—18 minutes

1   Travel freely from apparatus to apparatus and show me a still balance on each, using different body parts to support you. Plan also to try to include different methods of moving into your held position. You can jump, roll, swing, twist or lever.

2   Stay at your own starting group places to practise, improve, repeat and remember the following.

Ropes

Can you swing, let go at end of swing and land in a good balance position?

Boxes, mats, trestles

As a whole group, demonstrate a variety of balances and try to include a variety of levels, supporting parts and body shapes.

Inverted benches, mats

Balance walk forwards on bench, keeping some part of both feet touching the bench at all times. On the mats, can you balance, roll, balance?

Climbing frames

Follow your leader, travelling and holding still balances all over the frame.

Low box, bench, mats

Use the apparatus as spring boards from which to do an explosive high jump, followed by a beautifully controlled and balanced landing.

Mats

Show your partner your floorwork sequence of three balances with changing body shapes. Your partner will help you by suggesting one way in which to make an improvement.

Final Floor Activity
2 minutes

Jump up on the spot and land in excellent balance; run a short distance and land, well controlled in a good 'firm' balance.

Teaching notes and NC guidance
Development over 4 lessons

NC elements being emphasised:

a   Balancing, both on floor and apparatus.
b   Adopting good posture and the appropriate use of the body.

Floorwork

Legs

Balance is helped by landing with one foot after the other and keeping feet apart. This 'One...two' controlled, quite slow landing helps produce a nicely balanced finish. Stretched arms forwards or sideways also help balance and make the movement look good and 'gymnastic'.

Body

A contrast between the static, held balance and the rolling, rocking, tilting, levering, moving link movements is to be encouraged.

Arms

If elbow balance is too difficult, ask for a 'two count bunny jump', trying to hold it for two seconds with straight arms under shoulders under hips, and knees well bent to keep centre of gravity low.

Apparatus Work

'Can you visit all six different sets of apparatus, and each time, balance on a different part or parts of your body?'

Ropes
Build up to letting go by holding on and landing, to start with. Then let go with one hand, and finally, both hands.

Boxes, mats, trestles
Group activity which looks particularly good when all move into, hold and move out of balance together.

Inverted benches, mats
'Feel for bench. No looking down. Keep part of both feet in contact with the balance bench.'

Climbing frames
Note your leader's actions, body parts involved in travelling. In the balances, look out for body parts supporting and the clear body shape held.

Low box, bench, mats
Explosive high jumps can be after run or from standing on box or bench. Show good body tension to land firm and under control, with no wobbling.

Mats
Teaching partner will remember to 'Teach only one improvement at a time.'

Final Floor Activity

Jump on the spot will be from both feet to both feet. The jump after the short run can be from one foot or both feet to one foot after the other, or to both feet together or apart.

Year 4

Lesson Plan 9 • 30–35 minutes
May

Theme: *Swinging as an impetus and aid to movement.*

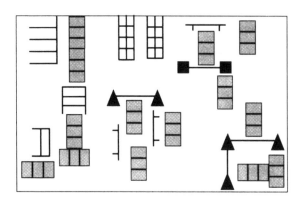

Floorwork
12–15 minutes

Legs

1   Practise swinging into an upward jump on the spot with a long pull upwards of the arms. Including arms above head, stretch everything strongly

2   Let ankles stretch strongly in the air and 'give' for a soft, quiet landing.

3   Change to a soft run into a strong swing into an upward jump. (With arm and/or leg.)

4   Now show me a swing into your upward jump on the spot, then your short run and swing into an upward jump. Land, well balanced, helped by arms stretched forwards or sideways.

Body

1   Sitting, curled up small, can you roll back and forwards? Swing back on to hands and shoulders with your upper body. Swing forwards to curled up sitting with a long swing of your legs. (Long straight legs give excellent swing.)

2   Can you roll from side to side on your back, curled up small? The swing will come from the arms and legs.

3   Can you swing left, then right, then a big swing to left and right over on to front and on to back again? Keep curled up small, with head on to knees.

Arms

Starting with arms above head can you try a long, slow swing up into handstand? After a few practices, try the quicker, shorter swing up with one leg. To help your balance on hands, try to make a straight line with your legs, like a tight-rope walker's pole.

Apparatus Work
16–18 minutes

1   Travel on floor and mats only. Can you show me swings into jumps on the floor, across mats or over low apparatus?

2   When you come to a mat, can you swing into a forward, sideways or backward roll?

3   Supporting your body on hands only, can you swing legs off the floor? Bent legs are easier to lift than straight ones.

4   Can you swing arms and/or a leg to bring you on to apparatus? Swing up and off with a stretched jump and a nice, squashy landing.

5   Stay at your starting group place in fives or sixes to repeat, practise, improve and remember the following:

   a   Start and finish on the floor away from the apparatus. Travel up to, on, along and away from the apparatus.

   b   Include swings into jumps on floor, on to and from apparatus.

   c   Roll on mats, including rolling from sitting or crouching on benches or low boxes.

   d   Take weight on hands after a long arm swing or a short leg swing.

Final Floor Activity
2 minutes

Follow your leader's travelling and swinging into a jump.

Teaching notes and NC guidance
Development over 4 lessons

NC elements being emphasised:

a Exploring different means of swinging, and practising and refining these actions both on the floor and on apparatus.

b Making judgements of performances and suggesting ways to improve.

Floorwork

Legs

1 Do a preparatory settling and bending in knees and swing of arms to rear before the powerful swing up into jump.

2 The arm swing aims to help the drive given by the ankle joints which should be fully stretched with toes pointing to floor.

3 The 'short run' only needs to be 3 or 4 strides. They experiment with one leg or one arm, or one of each, leading the swing up.

4 Ask observers at a demonstration 'Which part or parts do you think are most helpful in the swinging?'

Body

1 While rolling is the activity, 'feeling' the body parts that are swinging your weight, head and shoulders back, then feet forwards, is the emphasis.

2 Hands are clasped under knees and head is on to chest to make the body as rounded as possible.

3 A tight curl with no angles sticking out, and a strong sideways swing of the clasped hands and knees, are required to provide the momentum for a complete turn back to back lying.

Arms

Class will be equally divided in the two ways of swinging up on to hands. Let them find out their favourite, reliable method. The leg kick-up method is easier to control, quicker into position, and better for use on apparatus, later.

Apparatus Work

1 Standing, two-footed take-offs (across a mat, over a bench) will have a swing from both arms; walking or running take-offs will swing with one leg and/or arm.

2 'Feel' the leading, swinging parts in going into the rolls.

3 One leg can swing up behind you into a handstand. Two feet and legs can swing up into bunny jumps and handstands.

4 From a standing start, there will be much arm swinging on, and from, low apparatus. A good arm swing can also take you to standing or hanging on climbing frames and to hanging on ropes.

5 Plan the sequence under the headings 'pathways' from start on floor to finish on floor; 'rolls', including from being on apparatus; 'weight on hands' after swing of arms or leg. After *planning*, practising and *performing* your sequence, *reflect* on how it might flow more easily and smoothly. Throughout, be aware that the swinging into movement is the most important feature that we are trying to highlight.

Final Floor Activity

One behind the other, try to travel and swing in unison.

Year 4

Lesson Plan 10 • 30-35 minutes
June

Theme: *Dynamics (a) speed; slow, fast, speeding up or slowing down (b) effort; light, soft, firm, explosive (c) whole body tension in stillness, balance, flight and landing. All contribute to better looking, better controlled, more varied and demanding work.*

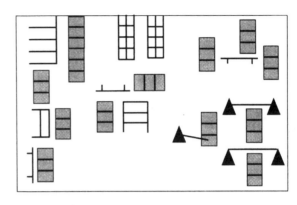

Floorwork
12—15 minutes

Legs

As you travel in a variety of ways using legs, can you plan to show me a contrast between some small, neat and light actions and some large, strong and lively actions?

Body

Balance still and stretch a part of your body firmly. From this 'firm' balance, can you relax and move on to another part of your body and balance strongly again? Stretch firmly those body parts that are not being used to support you, and aim for a three or four part sequence.

Arms

1   Travelling with arms and legs straight is strong work. Can you show me some examples of slow, strong work?

2   Arms and legs can be firm and straight in cartwheels.

3   They can also be straight while travelling on hands and feet. Can you experiment with the order of moving your four supports? Hands only, feet only; left side, right side; all at same time, bouncing forwards with a little lift off floor.

Apparatus Work
16—18 minutes

1   Travel to all parts of the room to visit as many pieces of apparatus as possible. Can you plan ways to cross the apparatus either quickly or very slowly?

2   Show me a 'firm' balance on apparatus with part or parts of your body stretched strongly. Relax, and move to a new piece of apparatus and demonstrate a new 'firm' balance on different supporting parts.

3   At your different groups can you plan how to do the following?

Climbing frames
Travel about the frame using arms strongly.

Ropes
Grip the rope so strongly with crossed feet that you can take one hand off at a time and start to climb. Or, swing and practise taking one hand off and then replacing it, to prove your good foot grip, without which you will never be able to climb.

Trestles
Travel with straight arms and legs above, below and across, and feel how strongly your body is working.

Upturned bench, trestle, box
Balance as a whole group to show me a variety of supporting parts and levels. All relax at the same time as your leader and move on to your next piece of apparatus.

Bench, box
Make a flowing sequence of travelling, rolling and jumping movements.

Mats, bench
Demonstrate slow and fast and/or gentle and explosive movements on apparatus and surrounding floor space.

Final Floor Activity
2 minutes

Run, accelerating into an explosive upward leap. Can you land, slowing gently to a stop?

Teaching notes and NC guidance
Development over 4 lessons

NC requirements being emphasised:

a Emphasising changes of speed and effort through gymnastic actions.
b Working vigorously to develop strength, suppleness and stamina, and to exercise the heart and lungs strongly.

Floorwork

Legs

The contrasting changes of speed and effort are movement qualities which enhance the appearance of a sequence, and make it look more polished. Easy, quiet, soft, gentle contrasting with strong, vigorous, firm, lively.

Body

If the class are asked to copy the teacher's sagging, limp, lazy balance, then the teacher's firm, strong, fully stretched one with good body tension, they will appreciate and understand which one is hard work to perform, strong, physical and attractive.

Arms

1 With front, back or side towards the floor, travelling on straight arms and legs is very hard work, even harder as the hands and feet move further apart.

2 Cartwheel travel counts because both feet and hands are main supporters during the action.

3 Hands only can travel forwards with straight arms, then stop with body almost straight. Feet can walk forwards, alternately, or they can spring forwards to land astride feet, depending on the springer's strength and suppleness.

Apparatus Work

1 A momentary touch on apparatus, as you move quickly on to the next piece, can be with one or both feet or hands, crossing by rolling, vaulting, jumping, twisting, swinging, circling.

2 Once again, only a momentary pause on each piece of apparatus, before moving off to hold a new firm balance, nicely stretched on a different body part. Demonstrate with good ideas for supporting parts, other than the usual ones on feet, or hands and feet.

Climbing frames
Strong hanging, pulling, lowering, circling and rotating, balancing.

Ropes
Pupils can practise the crossed foot action, sole over instep, sitting on the floor, without a rope. The teacher can help by putting hands under someone's crossed feet on the rope.

Trestles
Hanging, swinging, pulling, circling, high crawling.

Upturned bench trestle, box
A team balance, ideally following leader's timing – on, balance firm, relax, off and away to next one.

Bench, box
Flowing, easy, relaxed, calm sequence, almost nonstop.

Bench, mats
Slow and fast, gentle and explosive are the extremes of contrasting, eye-catching movements. Demonstrate good examples and ask the observers 'Look out for and tell me which pairs of contrasting movements pleased you the most.'

Final Floor Activity

Stillness; slow start into high speed run and dynamic leap; into slow motion landing; to a still finish.

Lesson Plan 11 ● 30-35 minutes
July

Theme: *Partner work which provides new experiences not possible on one's own; extends movement understanding because you need to be able to repeat your own movements and be able to recognise your partner's movements; and develops desirable social relationships.*

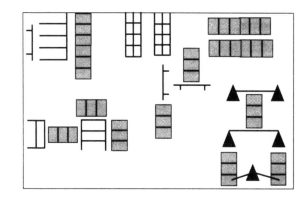

Floorwork
12–15 minutes

Legs

1 Follow your leader who is planning to show you three or four different travelling actions.

2 Aim to repeat each action a set number of times, so that you develop to travelling in unison.

Body

1 One partner holds a clear, 'firm' body shape which the other copies. Move from held shape to new held shape.

2 Can you plan linking movements which you are both able to perform (rolls; twists; jumps; stretches; etc.)?

Arms

Show me work on your hands, only, where there is a contrast. For example, one can be long and stretched, one can be tucked up small; one can swing slowly up into position with a long arm movement, one can kick up quickly.

Apparatus Work
16–18 minutes

1 Follow your leader, using only floor and mats to start with. Show your following partner how to cross, go under, along or around the apparatus without touching it. Plan a variety of travelling actions.

2 New leader, show your partner one touch only on each piece of apparatus, then off to the next piece. Plan a variety of 'one touches'.

3 At your different apparatus places, can you plan now to do the following?

Climbing frames
Mirror each other's movements on facing frames, and emphasise the pathways you travel along. Are you travelling vertically, horizontally, diagonally, weaving through spaces?

Ropes, bench
Side by side, build up to a matching sequence which can include climbing, swinging, rolling, jumping.

Trestles
Start at opposite ends of the apparatus. Approach, meet, pass and finish in your partner's starting place.

Boxes
One partner travels and stops. The other partner follows and catches up.

Benches
Follow your leader who will show you some work on legs only; then some work on hands and feet only; then some flight and rolls.

Mats
Follow your leader to include a straight pathway on one pair of mats and a zig-zag pathway on the other pair.

Final Floor Activity
2 minutes

Facing each other, one mirrors the other who leads in a 16 count jump routine which includes 4 sets of simple jumps. For example, feet together, 4; feet apart, 4; feet parting and closing, 4; feet together, turning right around for 4.

Teacher notes and NC Guidance
Development over 4 Lessons

NC elements being emphasised:

a Working safely, alone and with others.
b Making appropriate decisions and planning their responses.
c Practising, adapting, improving and repeating longer and increasingly complex sequences of movement.

Floorwork

Legs

1 Follow 2 metres behind partner to be able to see clearly:

   a   the actions;
   b   exact uses of body parts concerned;
   c   body shapes;
   d   directions.

2 Building up the sequence, action by action, rather than going into three or four different actions, straight away, will help. This build-up can happen over several weeks if pupils keep the same partners.

Body

1 'A' performs, 'B' copies, after observing;

   a   the supporting body parts;
   b   the whole body shape;
   c   the linking movements, in that order.

2 Leaders have to make allowances for their partner's ability, and include linking movements that they can obviously manage.

Arms

Ask for simple examples. Bunny jump, landing on same spot; bunny jump that takes you to a new floor space; long, wide cartwheel, travelling; handstand on the spot with bent legs.

Apparatus Work

1 Follow your leader, 2–3 metres apart, copying leader's actions as he or she negotiates the apparatus, without touching it. Visit all parts of the room, and be aware of others sharing the space.

2 New leader has to 'make decisions quickly', as he or she approaches each new piece of apparatus. What 'quick on and off' actions and uses of body parts are appropriate?

Climbing frames
Remember to show your partner a thumbs under, fingers over grip on the bars for a safe, strong, grip.

Ropes, bench
Side by side with great contrasts of still start and finish, swing through space, smooth roll and a lively jump.

Trestles
Negotiating each other is easier with one stationary and one going under, over or around, at passing place at centre.

Boxes
A series of travels and stops with following partner checking on actions, uses of body parts, body shapes and directions. Keep each part short and uncomplicated.

Benches
If kept simple and using one example only, each time, your partner will be able to shadow you, throughout.

Mats
Jumps and rolls lend themselves to straight and zig-zag pathways.

Final Floor Activity

Pairs will be praised and asked to demonstrate in this activity because they perform exactly in unison, and, more importantly, their ankles full stretching and bending is admirable and quiet.

Dance

The Aims of Dance

Education has been described as the 'structuring of experiences in such a way as to bring about an increase in human capacity.' Dance aims to increase human capacity under the following headings:

1 **Physical development**. We focus on body action to develop skilful, well-controlled, versatile movement. We want our pupils to move well, looking poised and confident. The vigorous actions in dance also promote healthy physical development, fitness and strength.

2 **Knowledge and understanding**. Pupils learn and understand through the combination of physical activity (with its doing, feeling and experiencing of movement) and the mental processes of decision-making, as they plan, refine, evaluate and then plan again for improvement.

3 **Enjoyment**. Dance is fun and an interesting, sociable, enjoyable physical activity. In addition to the perspiration and deep breathing which the vigorous physical activity inspires, there should be smiling faces expressing enjoyment. When asked why they like something, pupils' first answer is usually 'It's fun!' It is hoped that enjoyable, sociable and physical activity experienced regularly at school in dance and other physical education lessons, can have an influence on pupils' eventual choice of lifestyle, long after they have left school. We want them to understand that regular physical activity makes you look and feel better, and helps to make you feel relaxed, calm and fit.

4 **Confidence and self-esteem**. Particularly at primary school, a good physical education that recognises and praises achievement can enhance an individual's regard for him or herself, and help to improve confidence and self-esteem. Dance lessons are extremely visual and offer many opportunities to see improvement, success and creativity; demonstrating these admirable achievements to others; and helping pupils feel good about themselves.

5 **Social development**. Friendly, co-operative social relationships are part of most dance lessons. Achievement, particularly in the 'dance climax' part of the lesson, is usually shared with a partner or a small group. Pupils also share space sensibly with others; take turns at working; demonstrate to, and watch demonstrations by, others; and make appreciative, helpful comments to demonstrators and partners.

6 **Creativity**. It has been said that 'if you have never created something, you have never experienced satisfaction.' Dance is a most satisfying activity, regularly challenging pupils to plan and present something original. Opportunities abound for an appreciative teacher to say 'Thank you for your demonstration and your own, original way of doing the movements.'

7 **Expression and communication**. In dance we communicate through the expression in movement of the feelings or the action. We use, for example, stamping feet to express anger; we skip, punch the air or clap hands to show happiness; we swagger, head held high, to express self-assurance. Similarly, we create simple characters and stories by expressing them through movements associated with them. The old or young; machine or leaves; puppet, animal or circus clown, can all be expressed through their particular way of moving.

8 **Artistic and aesthetic appreciation**. Gaining knowledge and understanding of the quality-enhancing elements of movement is a particular aim of dance. Such understanding of quality, variety and contrast in the use of body action, shape, direction, size, speed and force, is a major contributor to appreciation of good movement. We want our pupils to understand what is good about good movement.

Stimuli as Starting Points with Which to Inspire Dance Action

Stimuli are used to gain the interest of the class, provide a focus for their attention, get them into the action quickly, and inspire in them a desire for movement.

A dance stimulus is something you:

○ **enjoy doing**, such as natural actions. Pupils will immediately start to walk, run, jump, skip, hop, bounce or gallop, whether accompanied by music, percussion, following the teacher/leader, or responding to an enthusiastic teacher calling out the actions.

○ **can hear**. Sounds that stimulate movement include:

a   medium to quick tempo music, including folk dance music

b   percussion instruments – tambourine, drum, cymbal, clappers

c   body contact sounds – clapping hands, stamping feet, slapping body, clicking fingers

d   rhythmically chanted phrases, words, place names or actions which can be shortened or elongated to inspire and accompany actions

e   vocal sounds to accompany actions, on the spot and travelling as in 'toom, toom, toom' marching; 'boomp, boomp, boomp' bouncing; and 'tick, tock, tick, tock' slow stepping

f   action songs, chanted rhymes and nursery rhymes.

○ **can see or imagine**. Objects like a leaf, branch, balloon, ball, bubble, puppet, rag doll, firework, can all be used to suggest movement ideas to children. Use of imagery and imagination helps to communicate what we are trying to express more clearly. 'Can you creep softly and slowly, as if you did not want to be heard, coming home late?'

○ **have seen on a visit, on television, or in a photograph**. Of particular interest to pupils are:

a   zoo animals – penguins. elephants, dolphins, monkeys

b   circus performers – jugglers, clowns, trapeze artists, acrobats, tightrope walkers

c   seaside play – swimming, paddling, making sandcastles, plus movements of the waves

d   children's playground activities – climbing, swinging, sea-saw, throwing and catching, skipping, circling on a roundabout.

○ **experience seasonally** – spring and growth, summer holidays, autumn and harvest, winter snow and frost, Guy Fawkes' Night, Halloween, Christmas toys, circus and pantomime, Easter eggs.

○ **consider newsworthy or of human interest** – Olympic Games, extremes of weather, newly arrived pupils, hobbies, family, friendship, approaching holidays.

Whatever the starting point, the teacher must convert it into the language of movement. Children cannot 'be' leaves, but they can 'Travel on tip toes with light, floating movements, tilting and turning slowly.' They cannot 'be' clowns, but they can 'Do a funny walk on heels, spin round with one leg high, fall down slowly, bounce up and repeat.' They cannot 'be' machines, but they can 'Try pushing down actions, like corks into bottles, on the spot, turning or moving along, as on an assembly line.'

The Creative Dance Lesson Plan

Warming-up Activities which start the lesson are important because they can create an attentive, co-operative, industrious and thoughtful start to the lesson, put the class in the mood for dance, and encourage them to move with good body poise and tension, sharing the floor unselfishly. The activities need to be simple enough to get the whole class working, almost immediately, often by following the teacher who, ideally, is a stimulating **'purveyor of action'** enthusiastically leading the whole class, often by example, into wholehearted participation in simple activities which need little explanation. Some form of travelling, using the feet, is often the warming-up activity, with a specific way of moving being asked for. It might be to show better use of space, greater variety, greater control, good poise and body tension, or simply an enthusiastic use of all the body parts to warm up.

The Movement Skills Training middle part of the lesson is used to teach and develop the movement skills and patterns that are to be used in the new dance. Here, the teacher is an **educator**, informing, challenging, questioning, using demonstrations and sometimes direct teaching.

a   Kneel down and curl to your smallest shape. Show me how you can start to grow, very slowly. Are you starting with your back, head, shoulders, elbows or arms? Show me clearly how you rise to a full, wide stretch position.

b   If gesturing is like speaking with your body's movement, how might your body gesture say 'I am angry'? Stamp feet, clench fists, punch the air, jump up and down heavily.

c   How are bubbles (made by teacher and pupils) moving? Where are they going? Floating gently, gliding smoothly, soaring from low to higher, sinking slowly.

The creating and performing Dance Climax of the lesson is the most important part and must not be missed out or rushed. If necessary, earlier parts of the lesson should be reduced. Here the teacher is a **coach**, helping and guiding the pupils as they work at their creation, moving round to all parts of the room to advise, encourage, enthuse, praise and, eventually, demonstrate.

a   Slowly, start to grow and show me which parts are leading as you rise to your full, wide flower shape in our 'Spring Dance'. You might even twist your flower shape to look at the sun.

b   Find a partner for our 'Gestures' dance and decide who is asking a favour by gesturing with body actions to say 'Please! I'm desperate! I need it! I must have it!' The other partner's body actions are saying 'Never! You must be joking! Go away!' When we look at demonstrations later, we will decide who the most expressive winners are.

c   For our 'Bubbles dance', I will say the four actions that are to be practised – floating gently, gliding smoothly, soaring, sinking slowly, and you will show me how you have planned to dance them.

Depending on its complexity, a dance lesson will be repeated three or four times to allow sufficient time for repetition, practice and improvement to take place, and a satisfactory performance to be achieved and presented.

It has been said that 'dance is all about making, remembering and repeating patterns.' Whether we are performing a created dance or an existing folk dance, there will still be a still start and finish, and an arrangement of repeated parts within.

The Traditional Folk Dance Lesson Plan – 30 minutes

Warming-up activities – 5 minutes

These varied steps can relate to the new figures to be taught, or they can be travelling steps or steps on the spot of any kind, to stimulate quick, easy enjoyable action to put the class in the mood for dance. The warm-up can be done alone or with a partner. As well as inspiring action, the teacher establishes high standards of neat footwork and good, safe, unselfish sharing of space. For example, 'Skip by yourself, to visit all parts of the room, keeping in time with the music.' 'When drum sounds twice, join hands with the nearest person and dance together.' 'When drum sounds once, dance by yourself again.'

Teach figures of new dance – 14 minutes

Teaching is easier in a big circle formation where everyone can see and copy the teacher. Often, all can perform the whole dance together, slowly and carefully, figure by figure, practising it to the teacher's voice, then doing it at the correct speed. The teacher's non-stop vocal accompaniment, along with the actions, serves to remind the class of the actions and keeps them moving at the correct speed. For example, 'Everyone ready... Skip to the centre, 2, 3, turn on 4; back to places, 2, 3, arrive on 4. Boys to centre, 2, 3, turn on 4; back to places, 2, 3, there on 4. Girls to centre, 2, 3, turn on 4; back to places, 2, 3, hands joined on 4. All circle left, 2, 3, 4, 5, 6, back the other way; circle right, 2, 3, 4, 5, 6, ready to start again.'

Teaching in sets of two, three, four or more couples is more difficult because the sets are separate, with someone's back to the teacher. Each leading couple in turn will be taken slowly through the figures, then walking, then dancing to the music or the teacher's vocal accompaniment.

Teach the new dance – 7 minutes

Ideally, the new dance will be performed without stopping, helped by early reminders to the next dancers from the teacher's continuous vocal accompaniment. It is sometimes necessary to stop the music after each dancing couple has completed the dance, because of problems experienced by some of the dancers. The new couples are put in position, the music is re-started, and they do the dance once again.

Revise a favourite dance – 4 minutes

This last dance, often chosen by pupils, should be a contrast to the lesson's new dance, for variety. A lively circle dance, with all dancing non-stop, can be contrasted with a set dance where only one or two of the four couples are dancing at a time.

Teaching Dance With 'Pace'

High on the list of accolades for an excellent dance lesson is the comment that 'it had excellent pace' and moved along, almost non-stop, from start to finish. Lesson pace is determined by the way that each of the several skills making up the whole lesson is taught. For example:

1 **Quickly into action**. Using few words, explain the skill clearly and challenge the class to begin. 'Show me your best stepping, in time with the music. Begin!' This near-instant start is helped if the teacher joins in and works enthusiastically with them.

2 **Emphasise the main teaching points, one at a time, while class is working**. The class all need to be working quietly if the teacher is to be heard. 'Visit all parts of the room – sides, ends and corners, as well as the middle.' 'Travel along straight lines, never following anyone.' (Primary school pupils always travel in a big anti-clockwise circle, all following one another, unless taught otherwise.)

3 **Identify and praise good work while the class is working**. The class teacher does not say 'well done' without being specific and explaining what is praiseworthy. Comments are heard by all and remind the class of key points. 'Well done, Emily. Your tip toe stepping is lively and neat.' 'Liam, you keep finding good spaces to travel through. Well done.'

4 **Teach for individual improvement, while the class is working**. 'Ben, swing arms and legs with more determination, please.' 'Lucy, use your eyes each time you change direction to see where the best space is.'

5 **Use a demonstration, briefly**, to show good quality, or a good example of what is expected and worth copying. 'Stop, please, and watch Olivia, Michael, James and Ravinder step out firmly with neat, quiet footwork, never following anyone.' 'Stop and watch how Chloe is mixing bent, straight and swinging leg actions for variety.'

6 **Very occasionally, to avoid using too much activity time, a short demonstration is followed by comments from observers**. 'Half of the class will watch the other half. Look out for and tell me whose stepping is neat, lively and always well spaced. Tell me if someone impresses you for any other reason.' The class watch for about 12 seconds and three or four comments are listened to. For example: 'James is mixing tiny steps with big ones.' 'Maisie is stepping with feet passing each other, then with feet wide apart.' Halves of the class change over and repeat the demonstrations with comments.

7 **Thanks are given to all the performers and to those who made helpful, friendly comments**. Further practice takes place with reminders of the good things seen and commented on.

A Pattern for Looking at and Developing Dance Movement

To avoid confusing him or herself and the class, the teacher will be thinking about, looking for and talking about one element within dance at a time. If, in the early stages of a lesson's development, the teacher is only looking for the actions and how the body parts concerned are performing them, there is some hope for progress and improvement. If, on the other hand, the teacher is exhorting the class to think about 'your spacing, actions, shape, speed – and what about some direction changes?', all at the same time, then confusion will be the only outcome.

Stage 1 The Body

What is the pupil doing?

1 **Actions**   travelling, jumping, turning, rolling, balancing, gesturing, rising, falling, etc..

2 **Body parts important**   legs, feet, hands, shoulders, head, etc..

3 **Body shape**   stretched, curled, wide. twisted, arched.

Stage 2 The Space

Where is the pupil doing it?

1 **Directions**   forwards, backwards, sideways.

2 **Level**   high, medium, low.

3 **Size**   own, little, personal space; whole room, large general space shared with others.

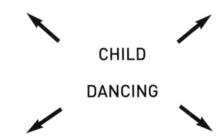

CHILD

DANCING

Stage 3 The Quality

How is the pupil doing it?

1 **Weight or effort**   firm, gentle, vigorous, light, heavy.

2 **Time or speed**   sudden, fast, slow, speeding up, slowing down, explosive.

Stage 4 The Relationships

With whom is the pupil doing it?

1 **Alone**   but always conscious of sharing space with others.

2 **Teacher**   near, following, mirroring, in circle with, away from, towards.

3 **Partner**   leading, following, meeting, parting, mirroring, copying, making contact with.

4 **Group**   circle, part of class for a demonstration

Headings When Considering a Pupil's Achievement and Progress Through Dance

Physical fitness

Strong, often prolonged physical activity, inspired by vigorous leg action, helps to promote normal, healthy growth and physical development. Lively leg action in dance also stimulates strong heart and lungs activity, leading to improved stamina.

Physical skill and versatility

Body management and self-control, called for in challenging situations, develops skill in natural actions such as travelling, jumping and landing, balancing, rolling, turning, rising and falling. When body management and self-control are good, there is an impression of poised, confident, versatile, safe movement.

Feeling valued and self-confident

Using their imagination, being creative, planning something original, and then sharing it with others, can develop and improve pupils' self confidence and self-esteem, particularly when the teacher and the class warmly and enthusiastically express their appreciation for the achievement. We want our dancers, eventually, to exude confidence and enthusiasm.

Expressing themselves

Using the body as an instrument of expression, and another way to communicate, pupils can express emotions, inner feelings, moods, convey ideas, and even create simple characters and stories. For many, this is a totally different, potentially eloquent outlet for expressing feeling as they stamp the work with their own personality.

Learning to develop friendly, co-operative, working relationships with others

Dance is the most sociable of physical education's activities. Working in pairs and groups; sharing space; taking turns; demonstrating and being demonstrated to; and appreciating and being appreciated by others, encourages desirable, enjoyable, co-operative social relationships.

Believing in the value of participation in physical activity

We want pupils to look and feel better after exercise, and believe that physical activity is enjoyable, and an essential antidote to the increasingly sedentary, inactive lifestyle of many people.

Becoming more competent, knowledgeable performers and spectators

Dance education develops an appreciation of the aesthetic and expressive elements within dance – variety and contrast in actions, shape, direction and level, speed, and degree of force.

National Curriculum Requirements for Dance – Key Stage 2: the Main Features

Programme of study   Pupils should be taught to:

a   create and perform dances using a range of movement patterns, including those from different times and cultures

b   respond to a range of stimuli and accompaniment.

Attainment targets   Pupils should be able to demonstrate that they can:

a   link skills, techniques and ideas and apply them accurately and appropriately, showing precision, control and fluency

b   compare and comment on skills, techniques and ideas used in others' work, and use this understanding to improve their own performance by modifying and refining skills and techniques.

Main NC headings when considering progression and expectation

Planning – This provides the focus and the concentrated thinking necessary for an accurate performance. Where standards of planning are satisfactory, there is evidence of:

a   the ability to think ahead, visualising what you want to achieve

b   good decision-making, selecting the most appropriate choices

c   a good understanding of what was asked for

d   an understanding of the elements of quality, variety and contrast

e   an unselfish willingness to listen to others' views and adapt own performance correspondingly.

Performing and improving performance – This is always the most important feature of a lesson. We are fortunate that the visual nature of Physical Education enables pupils' achievement to be easily seen, shared and judged. Where standards in performing are satisfactory, there is evidence of:

a   successful, safe outcomes

b   neat, accurate, 'correct' performances

c   consistency, and the ability to repeat and remember

d   economy of effort and making everything look 'easy'

e   adaptability, making sudden adjustments as required.

Linking actions – With a view to getting pupils working harder for longer, which is a main aim for Physical Education teaching, encourage them to pursue near-continuous, vigorous and enjoyable action, expressed ideally in deep breathing, perspiration and smiling faces.

Reflecting and evaluating – These factors are important because they help both the performers and the observers with their further planning, preparation, adapting and improving. Where standards are satisfactory, there is evidence of:

a   recognition of key features and keen and accurate observation

b   awareness of accuracy of work

c   helpful suggestions for improvement

d   good self-evaluation and acting upon these reflections

e   sensitive concern for another's feelings, and a good choice of words regarding another's work.

Year 4 Dance Programme

Pupils should be able to:

Autumn	Spring	Summer
1 Respond readily; dress well; and practise whole-heartedly to improve a performance. **2** Increase complexity of basic actions, step patterns and varied uses of body parts. **3** Respond to music, performing longer sequences, alone and with others. **4** Illustrate varied movement qualities, as in 'Autumn Leaves' use of space, shape, speed and tension. **5** Use vocal sounds to accompany and inspire actions, alone and with a partner. **6** Make up dances with a clear start, middle and ending. **7** Working with a partner, listen to, share and develop ideas. **8** Experience different pathways and shapes, leading and following a partner to use them. **9** Repeat, improve and remember longer sequences of repeating patterns of movement. **10** Celebrate Christmas in a 'Snow Dance' with its combination of teacher-led and pupil-created patterns. **11** Describe when elements of a dance are well performed.	**1** Enrich movements by varying shape, direction, speed and tension elements for variety and contrast. **2** Make rhythmic responses, through repeating patterns, to set tasks. **3** Use winter action words on cards as immediate stimuli to seasonal action. Partners can use percussion accompaniment. **4** Creatively link four figures from a selection of traditional dance figures with smooth flow and good teamwork, all in time with music. **5** Create characters by expressing them through the bodily movements associated with them. **6** Be able to repeat a series of movements remembered over a period of time. **7** Demonstrate a capacity for originality and an enthusiasm for using and presenting it. **8** Make simple judgements about own and others' performances, and suggest ways to improve. **9** Be found 'Working, not waiting; practising, not watching; and giving an impression of whole-hearted participation' at all times.	**1** Improve and refine content in dances with clear beginnings, middles and ends. **2** Work hard to develop own ideas and display independence of thought and action. **3** Be aware of good posture, always, and the correct use of the body when performing apparently simple actions. **4** Show control, poise and expression in use of gestures to demonstrate ideas, feelings and moods. **5** Learn a simple, international folk dance to improve class repertoire. Be able to improve, remember and repeat the dance, illustrating and describing its main features. **6** Contribute fully to partner and group activity, as a good listener and good planner, able to see ahead to the intended outcome. **7** Accompany 'Our Class Machine' dance with vocal sounds to inspire slow, quick, smooth, jerky, soft, heavy, straight and circular movements. **8** Exude vigour, poise, control, variety and contrast and an impression that 'This is easy.' **9** Be able to comment on a contrast in a pattern of movement.

Year 4

Lesson Plan 1 • 30 minutes
September

CD TRACK 2

Theme: *Basic actions.*

Warm-up Activities
5 minutes

1 Show me how quickly you respond to instructions and how good you are at finding spaces. Best walking... go!

2 Stop! This time, travel along straight lines, never in a circle (this is common, usually anti-clockwise, in primary schools). When I stop you, take one step, if necessary, to find a space by yourself.

3 Stop! Move to a better space. Well done, everyone.

4 Now show me your best, quietest, neatest running, still along straight lines, never following anyone. Go!

5 In your own big space, stop! Now, let's look at some examples of really good, quiet running, always looking for good spaces.

Movement Skills Training
15 minutes

1 Follow me through the eleven actions on my chart. I will use six beats of the music to each action. Keep with me: heels bouncing; whole body bouncing; walking forwards; walking backwards; skipping; running; running on the spot; stamping feet; clapping hands; clapping body parts; clapping hands with partner.

2 In our next practice of all the actions, work hard to make your shape strong and firm, with no 'saggy', lazy arms, legs or body.

3 Well done. Now sit down with a partner and plan a four-part sequence which must end with 'clapping hands with partner'.

4 Include a variety of actions, some on the spot, some travelling. A direction change provides an interesting contrast. When you have agreed, stand up and practise to the music.

Dance — Choose Four from Eleven
10 minutes

Music: Medium-to-quick, bouncy, rhythmic.

1 Let's all work together to my counting. Ready? Go! First action, 3, 4, 5 and change; second action, 3, 4, 5 and change; third action, 3, 4, 5 and change; clapping partner's hands, 4, 5, start again.

2 Stop! Well done. Decide now where you will go. Will you be one behind the other, side by side, or a mixture? Do you change direction somewhere? Do you part and close? Does one dance on the spot while the other travels (illustrated)? Ready to try again? Go!

3 Well done. I saw some excellent partnerships. Let's have half of the class looking at the other half. Look out for and tell me which pairs you like and why. Look for neat, quiet movements and pairs working and keeping together well – and maybe surprising you with their clever use of space.

Dance

Teaching notes and NC guidance
Development over 2 lessons

Pupils should be taught to:

a **recognise the safety risks of inappropriate clothing, jewellery and footwear.** Long trousers catch heels; watches and rings can impact against others and cause serious scarring and injury; large fashionable trainers are noisy, ungiving, often filthy, and should be banned indoors. Barefoot work is recommended because it is quiet, looks neat, and uses the small, under-used muscles of feet and ankles as they support, balance, propel and receive the body weight. Long hair should be bunched back to stop it impeding vision.

b **respond readily to instructions.** Now is the time, with a new class, to put a stop to bad behaviour, particularly if they do not respond immediately to instructions; rush around noisily, disturbing others; or do not try to move well, destroying any prospects for high standards.

Pupils should be able to show that they can practise, improve and refine performance. As well as the message 'This is the way we dress and behave in our Physical Education lessons,' the teacher should set the highest standards for the way that pupils participate. We want whole-hearted, vigorous and almost non-stop activity, inspired and guided by a well-prepared, enthusiastic teacher. Teaching will identify the features of good quality work; praise will encourage the praised to greater effort; and demonstrations of good work will set a standard to aim for. Deep breathing and perspiration, seldom experienced in the inactive lifestyles of many of today's youngsters, should be evident.

Warm-up Activities

1–5 With every new class it is essential to aim to stop the anti-clockwise travelling that all classes use, unless taught otherwise. By the end of this lesson the class should be travelling along straight lines, never curving around, never behind another's back.

Movement Skills Training

1 After the instant start with the music, the class listen to and copy each of the eleven simple actions, demonstrated by the teacher, which provide an excellent follow-up warm-up.

2 Stage one in improving the actions is to make the class aware of how the body parts concerned should be working. Firm shapes look good and show that you are working strongly.

3–4 Partners are asked to plan the four-part sequence, sharing the choices evenly and trying to provide variety and contrasting actions, ending sociably with 'partners clapping'.

Choose Four From Eleven Dance

1 The teacher's chanting keeps the class together. 'First action, 3, 4, 5, change! Second action, 3, 4, 5, change! Third action, 3, 4, 5, change! Clap hands, clap hands, start again!'

2 Having planned and remembered the actions of their sequence, partners are now asked to make the use of space more interesting and eye-catching. Their relationship if they travel, side by side; following a leader; one on the spot, one going around the other; parting and closing in many ways and directions, makes their 'partner togetherness' a strong feature, and an important one for a new class coming together in September.

3 Half-watching-half demonstrations, with follow-up comments by observers, is the climax.

Dance | Year 4 | Lesson 1

Lesson Plan 2 • 30 minutes
September

Theme: *Awareness of space.*

CD TRACK 1

Warm-up Activities
5 minutes

1   As you travel from space to space in time with my shaking tambourine, use some of the actions we met in the last lesson, or different ones such as gallop, slide, rush, creep, float, leap or hurry. Perform short travels and stop on the loud beat of the tambourine... go!

2   Use your eyes while you are still to look for your next good space. Variety in travelling actions, please. Go!

3   On each of the many stops, show me a well-balanced, whole body shape where parts of you reach out into the spaces in front, above, to the sides and behind you, high and low.

4   Well done, travellers and reachers into space.

Movement Skills Training
15 minutes

1   Stand in your own place, well away from anyone. Note where you are. There might be a mark on the floor, or you might be in line with a window or a door. Show me how your clever feet can travel away from your spot and return to the exact same place, exactly sixteen counts later. Go! 1, 2, 3, 4 (up to) 13, 14, 15, 16 and still!

2   Let's try again. Show me your varied actions and all the parts of the hall that you can visit in sixteen counts exactly. Go!

3   As well as visiting many parts of the room, can you reach out and touch the space around you, at different levels (high leaps, low slithering, medium arm-swing turns).

4   Now show me how many movements you can do in sixteen counts without moving away from your spot on the floor. Arms, legs, head, shoulders, and back can all bend, stretch, twist, reach, swing into all the spaces surrounding you.

5   Some movements, like a long stretching, can be slow, taking several counts. Others can swing or reach out quickly into space. Play around with the speed of your big body movements.

Dance — Space Travel
10 minutes

1   Find a partner and stand next to each other. Decide who will be number one and who will be number two.

2   While I sound out the sixteen counts, number one will move on the spot and number two will travel through space. Both will finish, still, in an attractive shape. Ready? Begin.

3   1, 2, 3... 13, 14, 15, 16, be still. Show me your firm shape.

4   Now number two will move on the spot and number one will travel. Be together again on count sixteen. Go! 1, 2, 3... 15... and still.

5   Let's spend a little time looking at our partner's actions on the spot, and then travelling. One can perform while the other watches and then we'll change over. This will help you to plan actions that are different to your partner's for variety.

6   Now, we'll do the whole thing twice through, working together.

7   Half of the class will watch the other half demonstrating. Look for and tell me about neat, varied movements and any really good examples of travelling for sixteen counts exactly.

Dance

Teaching notes and NC guidance
Development over 2 lessons

Pupils should be taught to be mindful of others. Space awareness is the same as awareness of other people. In a small room filled with fast moving pupils, it is essential to train the class to move safely, sensibly and co-operatively. The teacher often has to train the class not to travel around anti-clockwise, in a big circle, with everyone following and being impeded by others, typical in many primary schools. Accidents seldom happen with a class trained to travel on straight lines, visiting all parts of the room; never following the pathway of another; looking before changing directions; and sometimes running on the spot until a space appears.

Pupils should be able to show that they can repeat sequences with increasing control and accuracy. The requirement to practise, improve, remember and be able to repeat a series of linked movements is a main feature of the National Curriculum. Implicit in this is the need to be involved in the continuous process of thinking ahead to plan an intended outcome; then performing whole-heartedly in a focused, poised way, then reflecting on the success of the work as a guide to repeating the whole process.

Warm-up Activities

1 Pupils plan different actions to take them from space to space. Variety of actions and seeing where your next space is are the two main features.

2 The teacher can say 'I am looking at your feet and legs to see your many different actions, and I am looking at your eyes to check that you are really looking around you for good spaces.'

3 The challenge on the many stops is to be perfectly still, well-balanced, using full body shapes as you stretch, twist, reach into the space all around you, often with arms, but also with a leg.

4 The 'travellers and reachers into space' are all being trained in understanding and using own personal space and whole room, general space, shared with everyone.

Movement Skills Training

1–2 The teacher's tambourine and lively music, and the teacher's counting to start with, accompany the travelling away from and back to own floor position.

3 When the travelling away from and back to own floor spot is consistent, a request to add elevation into higher spaces and reachings to surrounding spaces is the next challenge.

4 Sixteen whole-body movements on the spot will use arms, knees, ankles, hips, shoulders and all the spine as they reach out to press against their pretend bubble of space.

5 Playing with the speeds of the movements will fill the hall with a mixture of ultra-slow and high speed, whole-body movements.

Space Travel Dance

1–4 The partners' space-travel dance is practised once through, to the teacher's counting, to a still position after their sixteen travels or moves on the spot. Places are changed for the next set of sixteen counts, aiming to travel or move well, using lots of floor and air spaces.

5–7 Using 32 counts, the dance is performed twice with each pupil performing both parts. The half-watching-half demonstrations, with comments, will inspire even better 'Space Travel'.

Lesson Plan 3 • 30 minutes
October

Theme: *Autumn.*

Warm-up Activities
5 minutes

1 In our last lesson your travelling was vigorous with strong steps, runs or jumps. Our movements on the spot were mostly firm stretching, bending, twisting or punching. Show me that you can also travel with light, gentle, floating movements – just like falling leaves in autumn. Lift up on to tiptoes and float, hardly moving, with arms and upper body tilting, turning slowly and gently. Keep going.

2 Pretend a gust of wind has just pushed you, making you glide more quickly along. Can your arms help you to glide and then tilt to curve around in a big, smooth turn?

3 The wind drops and the leaf drops, slowly floating down.

Movement Skills Training
10 minutes

1 Keep this feeling of lightness and let me see you swaying on the spot, almost floating in your own space. You may move one foot to give you a bigger reach out into space if you want. How far can you go forwards, back, or to the sides, just like a leaf still attached to its swaying branch?

2 Some movements will be jerky after a sudden gust of wind. Can you show me?

3 What is your leaf shape – wide, narrow, flat, curved, crinkly, twisted or jagged? Show me your flying movements and your shape, which might change in the wind, still attached to your branch.

Dance — Autumn Leaves
15 minutes

1 Our three-part dance will include: movements while attached to a branch; being blown from the branch and flying into space; and falling to the ground.

2 Let's all practise, one part at a time, using voice sounds as an accompaniment. On the branch, ready. Begin and wheeee... wheeee... gentle fluttering and turning and circling... wheeee.

3 Good, and I liked your sensible, gentle 'wheeee-ing'. Now the wind becomes stronger and stronger and blows the leaf, whoosh, out into space. Ready to fly... go... whoosh... whoosh... snap off... gliding, soaring, turning, hovering.

4 Very well done, again, with some excellent sharing of the air space in our hall. Now the wind has stopped and the leaves will slowly, softly, gently float to the ground. Can you slowly, softly, safely lower, bit by bit, to the floor?

5 Practise lowering to the floor again. Do not use your hands to support your fall. Flow, bending sideways along the sides of legs, hips and upper body, keeping your head and hands out of the way.

6 Half of the class work in the centre (the wood?), and half sit around the outside as wind machines. Watching half, please help by providing a gentle wind, then a stormy gusty wind, and then silence. Dancers, show me your favourite leaf shape as you wait to start. Wind blowers, please start.

7 For our change-over, the wind blowers can walk carefully through the fallen leaves, pretending to kick them, rolling them to the sides where they will sit up and become the new wind blowers.

Dance

Teaching notes and NC guidance
Development over 3 lessons

Pupils should be taught to adopt the best possible posture and use of the body. When we perform travelling actions the first thought is 'What is or are the leg actions I am using? How are my feet and legs working to do the action neatly and correctly?' When we perform whole-body movements, bending, stretching, twisting, curling or arching, our main thought is 'How am I holding and controlling my body posture and shape, particularly in the spine, head, arms and shoulders to represent and express the several movements.'

Pupils should be able to compose and control their movements by varying shape, size, level, direction, speed and tension.

Warm-up Activities

1 The mostly strong and firm travelling, jumping, bending, stretching, reaching of the previous lesson is to be followed by a different, contrasting movement quality throughout this lesson. The light, gentle, floating of leaves can be shown by someone dropping leaves from a height on the climbing frames for the class to observe and comment on, at the start of the lesson.

2–3 The use of imagery, to help understand a movement's force and effort quality, as with leaves in autumn, inspires more realistic gliding and soaring than simply being asked to glide or soar.

Movement Skills Training

1–3 The imagined leaves are still attached to the branch of the tree. Smooth, predictable, floating movements change to jerky ones suddenly in the wind, and leaf shape, as well as actions, are now considered and practised in the changing wind conditions.

Autumn Leaves Dance

1 The three-part, a: b: c, sequence has the same pattern as the leaves represented: movements, while attached to the branch; flight into space away from the tree; and the fall to the ground.

2 A vocal sound accompaniment is a good challenge, adding interest to movements that are gentle, quiet and not vigorous. Creative sound-making is an excellent stimulus, and good examples can be demonstrated and used by the class.

3 Wind sounds and leaf movements become stronger and the leaf suddenly snaps off into space. The fluttering, turning, rise and fall while on the tree becomes gliding, soaring, travelling/turning out in space.

4–5 Without wind, the leaves very slowly and gently start to drop, floating to the ground. This slow movement is as difficult as the lowering sideways drop to the floor, sagging sideways down through lower legs, upper legs, hips and seat, and all the upper body, with the head held well back, and hands out of the way, not taking any body weight.

6–7 The dance climax has half of the class unusually providing a vocal wind accompaniment while the other half perform the three-part dance. Each half will do both parts, observed closely while doing the leaf movements, and particularly expressive examples of leaf movements can be demonstrated, accompanied by sounds from everyone.

Lesson Plan 4 • 30 minutes
October/November

Theme: *Voice sounds.*

Warm-up Activities
5 minutes

1 Find a partner for a 'quick thinking' warm-up. Travel together to this bouncy music with one of you being leader this week.

2 The leader's first responsibility is to find good spaces and plan the varied actions to be copied by the partner.

3 When I bang the drum, make a change. It might be a different action, change of direction, or it might be a new position – side by side, following, one on the spot, one circling around, or holding one, two or no hands. (Several drum beats should be sounded about ten seconds apart to give time for the changes to take place.)

4 Well done, quick-thinking leaders. Watch these three couples whose quick responses and varied changes impressed me.

Movement Skills Training
15 minutes

1 Your 'wheeee-ing' and 'whooooshing' wind sounds in the last lesson also impressed me. Say together the words on my cards.
   SIZZLE – what pictures in your head does this word suggest? Show me how someone or something might move, if sizzling.
   ZOOM – what sort of action does this suggest? Slow or quick? If there is travelling, what will it be like? Show me (illustrated).
   BANG – what words could describe this action? Will it be slow or gentle, or not? Show me your ideas.
   BOING – what pictures, if any, does this word produce for you? What sort of action is 'boinging' like? Try to show me.

2 Keep practising by yourselves, moving to these words and saying them as you move. Try to express their speed and their force.

3 Re-arrange the order if you wish. Decide on a starting position that will be a good lead in to your first word. If you are moving like a rocket, motorbike, car, bullet, firework or whatever, try to show it in your starting position.

4 Let's have half the class looking at half the demonstrations to share good ideas. Look for good movement, actions that surprise you, and see if you can recognise what is being represented by the dancers.

5 After both sets of demonstrations and helpful, positive comments, there should be more class practice to let them use some of the good ideas and features seen and admired.

Dance — Sizzle! Zoom! Bang! Boing!
10 minutes

1 Find a partner and share your ideas to see if you can come up with a really good sequence, working together. Remember that it is not long; two of the actions, at least, are very short.

2 Are you going to say the words together, or will only one speak at a time? Together would be good, but how will you do it at exactly the same time?

3 Show good, clear actions and shapes and a change of direction, level, speed or force to make it even more interesting.

Dance

Teaching notes and NC guidance
Development over 3 lessons

Pupils should be able to:

a **respond to a range of stimuli through Dance.** As stimuli, the four words concerned provide a double bonus. They can each inspire specific images – rocket, bullet, explosion, firework, sausages frying – and the image can inspire the idea for the movement. They can also be given a strong vocal accompaniment which is most enjoyable and gives the sequence a rhythm.

b **compose and control their movements by varying shape, size, level, direction, speed and tension.** Pupils will first be asked 'Can you show me your clear, firm starting shape for your four-part sequence, the body shapes within the actions concerned, and then try to hold and show me your finishing shape.' They will then be told 'A change of level or direction at some point will give interesting variety. Low sizzling rocket to high flight; high, crashed motor-cyclist to lying down flat.' Finally, they can be asked to think about the 'How?' of their movement. 'Will your actions be slow or quick, gentle or explosive, light or heavy? Can you surprise me with a sudden contrast?'

Pupils should be able to show that they can work safely in pairs. The partner work is totally partner-centred. Pupils have full responsibility for deciding and planning their sequence, the order of the actions, and how 'together' they will be in performing and adding vocal sounds. They need to work safely, carefully and considerately, not crashing into or disturbing other pairs. They need to be willing to listen to and consider the views of their partner.

Warm-up Activities

1–4 Making the class listen for the drum beat, signalling 'Change your action!' is an excellent way to ensure an attentive start to the lesson. This is also a good guide for checking on their understanding of what can be 'different' in dance movement – actions; direction changes and uses of space; body shapes; relationships with partner; speed and use of body tensions. An 8–10-second practice of each action is enough to let following partner recognise, practise and remember it, before the next drum beat 'Change!' Observers of demonstrations are asked to 'Look at the three couples and tell me what action changes you particularly liked.'

Movement Skills Training

1–3 The previous lesson's experience of vocal sound making will have helped. Each word on the teacher's card is said by the class who are then challenged to suggest an associated movement suggested by each word. Questioning by the teacher aims to find 'The what?' and 'The how?' and usually produces many interesting, unusual and humorous responses.

4–5 A half-watching-half demonstration, here, will probably provide more totally unexpected responses than in most other lessons. Such originality in the thinking and the planning deserves the praise it will receive. Using body movements to express a character or a story requires clear actions, firm body shapes, good use of space, speed and effort.

Sizzle! Zoom! Bang! Boing! Dance

1–3 This is a shared partners dance, after deciding the order of the three words; the objects or persons expressed; and how they will say the words as a team. The answers to 'What actions?' and 'What shapes and effort?' will help to identify the subjects.

Lesson Plan 5 • 30 minutes
November

Theme: *Pathways and shapes.*

Warm-up Activities
5 minutes

1 Think of a shape or a letter in your name that you would like to draw on the floor in a tiny space, then repeat exactly using the whole floor space. When you have decided, let me see you walking your shape or letter, tiny, then room-size.

2 Return to your starting place after your long travel. Practise again, tiny and then as large as you can manage.

3 Can you use interesting travelling actions and neat turning, leaning or twisting into curving pathways? I am watching your feet taking you and your upper body guiding you.

Movement Skills Training
12 minutes

1 Don't rush into your answer! Think carefully. Can anyone be brilliant and tell me a number between 5 and 7?

2 Well done, Sarah, 6 is correct. Now, everyone, find a big space where you can travel and draw a capital 'S'. Show me your starting body shape and position. Will you lead with an arm, hand, shoulder or your back? You might even be starting, standing in an 'S' shape with rounded legs and back.

3 Travel along your curving 'S' pathway and then hold still. Once again, show me your neat, clear, curving travelling actions. Go!

4 Well done. I liked your curving movements. Now, show me your capital 'I', going straight like a bullet or an arrow to a space near you. You can start low and rise up, soaring like a glider or a bird. You can be wide like a wall with wide spread arms or legs, going sideways. You choose.

5 Ready for your 'I'? Go! And hold your finish, perfectly still.

6 Well done. That was very good and very varied. Now turn, step or jump into your capital 'X'. Which body parts are you crossing? You can be standing, kneeling or lying as you do this.

Dance — Think of a Number between 5 and 7
13 minutes

1 Find a partner and show each other your three 'S', 'I', 'X' ideas. Partner number one will go first. Ready? Go! Make 'S' and be still. Now make 'I' and be still. Now show your 'X'.

2 Your turn, partner number two. Ready? Go!

3 You and your partner are going to combine and do a 'follow the leader' version of what we have been doing. Discuss, decide and plan your three moves. Partner number one, 'the leader' will go first and stop. Partner two follows, copies and stops, and so on, through to a shared way of making your 'X'. Practise freely when you have decided your three actions.

4 Get ready, everyone, for your shared 'S', 'I', 'X' ideas. Number one, go! Number two... follow. Number one... go! Number two... follow. Now your shared 'X', go!

5 Once again, please, but this time you will set your own speeds. Show me your clear starting positions and shapes. Ready? Go!

6 Let's have half the class looking at a demonstration by the other half so that all these excellent ideas, particularly the 'Xs', can be shared. Watch and then tell me which couples you particularly liked and why.

Dance

Teaching notes and NC guidance
Development over 2 lessons

Pupils should be taught to:

a **respond readily to instructions.** This is an easy good fun dance capable of many levels of outcome, depending on the quality of pupils' attention as they are taken through each of the three stages of the dance. The leader's capital 'S' can be without focus, a nondescript, poor-quality movement, followed by an even less impressive partner. Or there can be an eye-catching starting shape, with a part of the body obviously about to lead, neat, wide, curving, travelling actions, clearly led by arm, shoulder, back, elbow or hip into an eye-catching, clear, still shape.

b **be mindful of others.** As a helpful, co-operative, sympathetic leader it is essential to repeat movements accurately so that your copying partner keeps seeing, for example, the same starting shape, travelling actions and parts leading into the curves. A sequence needs to be repeated for it to be practised, then remembered and presented. The following, copying partner needs to be equally co-operative, giving his or her whole attention to the leader's actions, to ensure a successful and repeatable performance.

Pupils should be able to show that they can make simple judgements effectively to improve the accuracy, quality and variety of the performance. Because the dance is so short, it is easy to arrange demonstrations of the partner work. Half of the class can watch the other half. Pairs can watch pairs. Observers are asked 'Please tell me which pairs you really liked. Tell me what it was that pleased you, so that you might all learn from it, and maybe include it in your own dance.'

Warm-up Activities

1–3 In drawing a letter of their name, they are told 'Remember your travelling actions; which parts of you are leading as you go; and your starting, travelling and finishing body shape. The lesson is about the pathways we travel along, and our body shapes.'

Movement Skills Training

1–6 Everyone works at drawing the letters of 'SIX', travelling slowly from a starting position, emphasising the curve shape of the 'S'. The teacher suggests ways to travel to represent the letter 'I', direct, in contrast with the curving 'S'. 'X', drawn on the spot, involves making whole body, cross shapes with arms, legs and spine. 'What travelling actions and body parts lead for your "S"? What are you doing for your straight "I"? What body parts crossing make your "X"?' are continually being asked.

Think Of A Number Between 5 and 7 Dance

1–6 Each leader thoughtfully tries hard to make the three parts of the dance more clearly expressed by the repetitions of the clear body shapes and the starting, travelling 'S'; the identifying of the object and its distinct travelling on 'I'; and the body parts used in forming the 'X'. Each watches the other, initially, before deciding on the three favourite actions to be used by partners. During the practices by individuals and the eventual, joint performances, the teacher will set the speed of the dance to keep the whole class together. 'Number one, S, go! Number two, follow! Number one, I, go! Number two, follow! Both, X, go!'

Lesson Plan 6 • 30 minutes
December/January

CD TRACK 23

Theme: *Christmas and midwinter snow.*

Warm-up Activities
5 minutes

1   In our last lesson we used our bodies to draw the word 'S', 'I', 'X'. Can you now use your bodies in big, lively, warming-up actions to show me the special present you might like for Christmas. I don't want any sitting down, video watching, thank you! Let's pretend there's a prize for the biggest, most physical and imaginative performance. Go!

2   Try to make a repeating pattern. I'll do a golf swing forwards; swing back; swing forwards; and drive my golf ball out of sight!

3   Keep working. I see lots of good actions: team games; cycling; flying kites; gliding; canoeing; judo with an imaginary partner.

Movement Skills Training
17 minutes

Music: *Sleighride* from *Leroy Anderson Favourites* by Saint Louis Symphony Orchestra (2 mins 47 secs)

Time	
0 secs	All start in a relaxed position, sitting, kneeling or crouching. Ben and Emma will stand until the music starts, then walk about, waving, 'It's snowing. Come out to play.'
12 secs	All move around, marvelling at the beautiful snowflakes. Catch them at high, medium and low levels. Rub your hands together or against your clothes. Reach and catch more.
28 secs	Make footprints in the snow. Choose to brush the snow gently, flicking it away, or make heavy, deep footprints.
44 secs	With your partner, crouch down to make a snowball. Face each other, starting with a small snowball. As it grows, rise up and make it bigger by rolling it sideways.
1 min 3 secs	We skate now with the inexpert, awkward number ones going first. You stumble and throw up arms for balance.
1 min 11 secs	The expert number twos glide smoothly to all parts of the room – not a stumble anywhere.
1 min 20 secs	Inexpert, awkward group, try again. You are worse than ever and some of you even fall down.
1 min 28 secs	Expert group, perform even better, sliding gracefully, doing amazing twists and turns, and always in control.
1 min 36 secs	Kind experts, pick up your awkward partner, hold on to and lead them through some successful, neat skating.
1 min 45 secs	Sleigh arrives with presents for everyone. Catch a parcel, crouch down, unwrap it and then show off what you have received by playing with it. Big, whole-body actions, in a repeating, easy-to-remember sequence, please!
2 mins 20 secs	All move into an open circle in pairs behind two leaders and walk around, anti-clockwise.
2 mins 37 secs	The line of dancers starts to fall to the floor, with the rear pairs of dancers going down first. The leading pair fall on the last note of music at 2 mins 47 secs.

Dance – Snow Dance
8 minutes

Well done, everyone. Let's have another practice or two to help you remember all the parts and make them even better.

Dance

Teaching notes and NC guidance
Development over 4 lessons

Pupils should:

a **respond to music.** It helps to speed up the teaching of this dance if pupils are asked to find a partner and sit down near the source of the music. They are told that partner work will take place in two parts of the dance: the making of snowballs and the skating. Partners are asked to number themselves one or two for the skating. 'Listen to the music and I will tell you the actions that accompany each section. Imagine yourselves dancing to each section as I talk you through.' The teacher can also illustrate the different actions within the several parts to help the seated class imagine performing them. A confident teacher can then talk and lead the class through the dance, accompanied by the music, to give them a feel for the whole dance – its beginning, middle and end. Subsequently, each part of the dance can be taken, planned in greater detail, repeated, improved, developed and remembered.

b **create simple characters and narratives.** We 'create' or express someone or something through movements associated with the person or the object. Children catching snowflakes; making snowballs; tramping in the snow; ice skating; and playing with a favourite toy, are all expressed through whole-body movements, inspired by the teacher's asking 'What actions? What body shapes? Where are they doing it? How are they doing it?'

Pupils should be able to show that they can respond imaginatively to the various challenges. Almost total imaginative freedom is given to the class as they plan how to tiptoe or tramp through the snow; make an ever-increasing snowball; skate; and choose their favourite object for the middle part of the lesson. Brilliant, imaginative ideas are, of course, shared with, and often copied by, the observers.

Warm-up Activities

1–3 It is hoped that there will be lots of lively cycling, kicking of rugby and footballs, skating, skipping with ropes, and running and jumping to shoot basketballs. Making a 'repeating pattern' is important so that the sequence can be more easily remembered and repeated.

Movement Skills Training

Having explained the actions that take place from start to finish, the teacher can now start the music and give a running commentary for the class to respond to. The sitting start; the catching and playing with snowflakes; the making of heavy or light footprints in the snow; the making of the huge snowball with the partner; the skating brilliantly or ineptly; the catching of the gift parcel, can all be performed easily without stopping. The music should then be stopped so that everyone can decide what their present is, the teacher insisting that it has the potential for vigorous activity. 'This is a PE lesson. Be very active with your present. No mobile phones or computers, please!' After the practising of the three- or four-part repeating sequences, the music is re-started from the point at which it was stopped. The dance continues, with the teacher's reminder and accompanying commentary keeping the whole class together. For the very end of the dance, the teacher joins in, with a partner, to lead the big circle of pairs anti-clockwise around the room. 'Start falling to the floor in your pairs, starting with those at the back of our circle.'

Lesson Plan 7 • 30 minutes
January

CD TRACK 16

Theme: *Winter.*

Warm-up Activities
5 minutes

1. Let's split the class into two halves. Each half will skip to the folk-dance music for eight counts by itself. When not dancing, stand still. Number ones, go! 1, 2, 3, 4, 5, 6, twos get ready. Twos go, 2, 3, 4, 5, 6, 7 and change. Repeat several times.

2. Dancers, time your movements to touch hands with a non-dancer, on counts seven and eight and say 'Go!' to send them off. If you don't receive a hand touch, it doesn't matter. Go!

Movement Skills Training
13 minutes

1. In our last lesson we thought about winter and its snow. I want us to think, now, about some winter words and how we might express them in movement. Look at the five words on my card and think about three you might choose for your 'Winter Words' dance.
STAMP SHIVER FREEZE SLIP FALL

2. We will take each word in turn and try showing it in action, to make sure you understand it. Let me hear your suggestions for the kind of movement that best shows the meaning of the word.

3. What about 'Stamp'? On the spot or travelling; heavy; firm; quite slow because of heavy footwear; flat-footed; noisy.

4. 'Shiver'? Also on the spot or moving; shaking rapidly; whole body huddled in to oneself; twisting.

5. How can we dance 'Freeze'? It can be a winter word about water; a drip becoming an icicle; or it could be the dancer stiffening into a rigid shape.

6. Our inexpert dancers in the 'Snow Dance' slipped and stumbled out of control. 'Slip' can be a long, smooth action or a sudden move to end a dance.

7. 'Fall' can also be used to end a dance and is good fun in slow motion as the person or even the snowman melts or tumbles over.

Dance — Winter Words
12 minutes

1. You've all had a practice at the five words, showing them in movement. Sit beside your partner and study the list on my card. Decide which three words appeal to both of you the most.

2. Stand and practise your three words by yourself and see what you think is the best and most sensible order in which to perform them.

3. One of you go and collect a piece of percussion, sit down and watch your partner dancing your three words. Dancers, begin.

4. Dancers, sit down beside your partner. Listen to any advice to help you perform better. Then perform again, and your partner will quietly accompany you with the percussion, starting and stopping you, for each action.

5. Well done, dancers. Well done, musicians, with your friendly, helpful comments and your good, quiet accompaniment and timing.

6. Change places and we will repeat all the practising. (Without percussion; advice; repetition with percussion.)

7. Well done, everyone, once again. Now it's time for couples to look at others to see if you can identify the three actions.

Dance

Teaching notes and NC guidance
Development over 3 lessons

Pupils should be involved in the continuous process of planning, performing and evaluating with the greatest emphasis on the performing. Thinking about any Physical Education lesson in National Curriculum terms, the teacher should consider 'Am I providing opportunities and challenges for the class to plan thoughtfully before performing; perform in a focused, neat, poised way; and reflect on their own and others' performances to influence subsequent planning and performing?' Pupils are continually being challenged to 'Show me how you will move to demonstrate "Shiver". How are you planning to "Freeze"? What sort of "Slip" will I see if I watch you? Please plan thoughtfully, then practise'.

Pupils should be taught to respond to a range of stimuli, through Dance. Action words on cards are an excellent stimulus for getting a class moving quickly. When words can also stir the imagination with specific, topical ideas, performing becomes more clearly understood and easily visualised. The eventual dance outcome is for real, not just a piece of 'exploration'. Partner advice and observation are further stimuli, as is an enthusiastic, encouraging, appreciative teacher.

Warm-up Activities

1–2 This popular warm-up, danced to folk-dance music with eight-count phrases, demands the attention of the whole class as they travel, approaching someone to touch on counts 7 and 8, or as non-dancers, wait, ready to be hand-touched. The travelling has to be cleverly adjusted to ensure that you are in the right places (approaching a non-dancer) at the right times.

Movement Skills Training

1–7 The teaching is a mixture of questioning, asking about the nature of the actions on the card. 'Is this a light or heavy action? Where will it happen? Quiet or noisy? Why might you be doing this?' and teacher suggestions, 'Freeze might mean a stream, a drip from a roof or it could be how you are feeling.' Each word is examined and experienced and good examples are demonstrated and shared.

Winter Words Dance

1–2 'Find a partner. Sit down and think about the five words on my card. Work together to choose the three actions you would like to include in your eventual 'Winter Words Dance'. Each partner practises by him or herself to decide what is the best order for the words.

3–6 This pattern for learning a dance is often used – one partner sits with a tambourine to accompany the dancing partner; dancer performs, without sound accompaniment, the first time. Dancer sits down beside partner to be told something encouraging and something to improve the dance. After being coached, the same dancer repeats the actions, with a sound accompaniment. Dancers change places and repeat the above learning pattern of performing; being coached; repeating the performing.

Lesson Plan 8 • 30 minutes
February

CD TRACK 10

Theme: *Creative, traditional-style folk dance.*

Warm-up Activities
5 minutes

1 Follow your leader, two metres apart, copying the leader's actions. Lead your partner into good spaces and include three or four neat, quiet, contrasting actions. (Contrast, for example, small walking or running steps, hardly travelling, with a lively skip change of step or polka with good travel; gentle bounces on the spot with lively slipping steps sideways.)

2 Change leaders. New leader, keep the same actions, but try to add a change of direction and body shape somewhere. (For example, small steps, body stretched tall on tiptoes; lively, long skipping steps with well-bent knees and arms; little bounces turning on the spot; chasse side-steps to left and back to right with arms and legs parting wide and closing.)

Teach One-couple Figures to be Linked Creatively
15 minutes

Partner on left facing top is A. Partner on right is B. Each figure takes eight bars of the music.

1 Cast off to the side, A turning to the left, B turning to the right, and dance to the bottom for four counts, then turn in, meet, joining hands and dance to top and own places for four.

2 Advance and retire and change places. Partners dance towards each other for two counts, then back for two, then they go forwards again, giving right hands to change places. Now in your partner's place, you usually repeat this figure back to your places, giving left hands to change places. Can any of you suggest a different way to return, still lasting eight counts?

3 Dance around your partner and back. A dances around in front of B and back into place. B repeats around A, back into place. The person being danced around, can you do something on the spot as your partner goes around? For example, setting steps, turn to keep facing partner, or give a helping hand to partner, on count three, around to his or her place.

4 Practise your own eight-count figure that develops from the warm-up activities. For example, include one stationary and one travelling partner; partners parting and closing; or one performing on the spot and one travelling around in a circle.

Couples Plan and Practise Own 32-bar Dance
10 minutes

You may include one or two of your own ideas in your four-figure dance. The 'advance and retire', with your own ending, if chosen, will be half of the dance. Plan; practise; demonstrate; share ideas; receive comments; plan again; adapt; improve; practise; remember.

Dance

Teaching notes and NC guidance
Development over 3 lessons

Pupils should be taught to:

a **be physically active.** Folk-dance lessons should be among the most vigorous and physical because they have a continuous, repeating pattern, maintained by the musical accompaniment. The teacher's responsibility is to give clear, succinct explanations and demonstrations of the new figures or steps, and then let the class practise them.

b **be mindful of others.** 'Others' include other couples sharing the floor space with you, requiring you to restrict yourself to a space, sometimes less than you would like. 'Others' include partners dependent on your being in the right place at the right time (not early or, worse, late) for the successful completion of a figure. Being 'mindful' means that you will work hard, co-operatively and unselfishly with your partner in deciding on your joint created dance.

c **perform a number of dances from different times and places,** including some traditional dances of the British Isles. The set and the figures used in this lesson are typical in English and Scottish country dance.

Pupils should be able to show that they can repeat sequences with increasing control and accuracy. Being able to link together a series of movements is an important feature within the National Curriculum. It is easily achieved and practised in a folk-dance setting, with the pattern of four repeating figures and the rhythmic musical accompaniment.

Warm-up Activities

1–2 The 'partners co-operating' emphasis of the lesson begins straight away in the 'Follow the Leader' start. 'Contrasts' is an element that enhances quality in dance and partners are initially challenged to provide several contrasting actions for partners to recognise and copy. New leaders are asked to try to add direction and body-shape changes to the sequence being practised. Good use of space and shape are further examples of quality-enhancing features.

Teach One-couple Figures to be Linked Creatively

1–3 Each of the three figures is demonstrated first by the teacher and a partner, slowly, counting out the eight steps and emphasising back to 'own places on 8'. The teacher's chanting is a reminder of the actions. 'Cast off to own sides, 3, hands joined on 4; up the middle, 2, 3, back to places.' 'Forwards for 2, back for 2; right hands to change places, 3 and 4. Forwards for 2, back for 2; left hands to partners, change and back to own places.' 'Around your partner, 2, back to own places; new partners around, back to own places.'

4 The partner-created, eight-count figure starts with partners standing, facing each other, in the usual set positions.

Couples Plan and Practise Own 32-Bar Dance

Couples are reminded that the second figure practised, the 'advance and retire', is a 16-count figure and would be half of their whole dance, if included in their 32-bar dance. The practising of the created dance will be done to music so that the essential requirement, being in the right places at the right time, is also being practised. Good posture; neat, quiet footwork; and good partner 'togetherness' will be praised after demonstrations by couples.

Lesson Plan 9 • 30 minutes
March

Theme: *Traditional folk dance.*

Warm-up Activities
5 minutes

1 Stand with your partner in the A or B groups into which I have divided the class.

2 A group, you will start, travelling together for eight counts. While the As are travelling about the room, the B group will do a partner activity on the spot for eight counts (e.g. turning; advancing and retiring; one dancing on the spot, one dancing around the other; chasse one way for four counts and back for four).

3 Change over the actions for the next eight counts.

4 Continue, alternating travelling with a practice on the spot.

Half-Watch Half Demonstrating Their Two Sets of Figures
4 minutes

1 While you are watching, look out for and tell me which couples kept together, danced neatly and quietly, and were in time with the music at all times.

2 Thank you for your lively demonstrations and your friendly, helpful comments. Let's have another practice and try to use some of the good features that were admired.

Teach and Dance — Farmer's Jig
15 minutes

Music: Farmer's Jig or any 32-bar jig tune

Formation: Longways set of four couples.

Bars 1–8 All couples join nearer hands and walk to top of set for four counts. All turn and return to own places for four counts.

Bars 9–16 All couples join both hands and slip-step (quick chasse or gallop) to top of set for four counts. All turn and slip-step back to places for four counts.

Bars 17–24 First and second couples dance right and left hand star, while third and fourth couples do the same.

Bars 25–32 All face top of set where first couple cast off, A to the left, B to the right, others following. First couple make an arch at the bottom, others promenade up the centre to remake set with a new first couple who will repeat the dance.

Revise a Favourite Dance
6 minutes

This can be a folk dance such as 'Cumberland Reel' or 'Djatchko Kolo' or, for variety, a creative dance from a previous lesson, such as 'Snow Dance' or 'Think of a Number Between 5 and 7'.

Dance

Teaching notes and NC guidance
Development over 3 lessons

Pupils should be taught to:

a **be physically active.** Vigorous leg activity while travelling is a continuous feature of a folk-dance lesson, and the teacher should be aiming to fill the lesson with such action. Praise in the warm-up is for those demonstrating wholehearted and vigorous activity. In the easy dance, all four couples are kept busy throughout.

b **be mindful of others.** The important 'others' here are your partner and the three other couples making the long set with you. To maintain the continuous flow of the dance, all eight must watch what is happening and be ready to start each of the figures at the right time. The teacher should praise and demonstrate with a group 'whose excellent teamwork makes the dance run smoothly, with everyone performing non-stop.'

c **respond to music.** The eight-bar phrasing of the music is practised in the warm-up. The ability to keep in time with the music is praised in the demonstrations. Taking eight counts exactly for each figure of the four figure dance is continually emphasised. This is helped by the teacher's rhythmic accompaniment of the actions of each figure. 'Hands joined, walk to top; turn and back again...'

d **perform a number of dances from different times and places,** including some traditional dances of the British Isles. This English folk dance is simple and has a repeating pattern of four varied figures. The non-stop action for all four couples makes it a very lively, physical and sociable dance.

Warm-up Activities

1–4 The couples dancing on the spot, around whom the travelling couples dance, will need to be well spaced apart. Everyone will need to be aware of available floor space and travelling dancers might need to improvise by shortening strides or even dancing on the spot, for a moment, if they suddenly come to a crowded area. 'Partner activity on the spot for eight counts' is to be a single activity, repeated, and can be from the previous lesson, or something new.

Teach and Dance
'Farmer's Jig'

Bars 1–8 'Walk to top, 3 and turn; back to places, 3 and stop!' The walk makes this easy because they are not travelling very far. All should have been made aware of their own particular spot on the floor, to return to, as part of their long set.

Bars 9–16 In the previous figure, they walked, facing forwards, nearer hands joined. In this figure, with both hands joined with partners, they are side on to the direction they are travelling and the quick chasse steps (step, close, step, close) sideways are the easiest to control. In the four beats of the music each way, they will perform eight sideways chasse steps.

Bars 17–24 Once again, all dancers are performing, as they wheel around clockwise for four travelling steps, right hands joined with diagonally opposite dancer, and wheel back, anti-clockwise, with left hands joined. 'Right hand wheel, 3 and 4; left hands back, 3 and 4.'

Bars 25–32 The progression in this dance is used to take the original, first, top-of-set couple down to the bottom of the set to provide a new top-of-set first couple. The cast off to own sides and the joining of the first couple's hands to make the arch takes only four, brisk counts and travelling steps. Second to fourth couples going under the arch and returning to their new positons in the set, standing still, takes only four counts. Dance continues with new first couple.

Lesson Plan 10 • 30 minutes
March/April

Theme: *Circus.*

Warm-up Activities
5 minutes

1 Stand in a big circle, facing the centre, and start straight away with me. Skip to the centre, 3, 4; stay and clap hands for 4; chasse sideways out for 4. In your own starting places, show me a favourite action on the spot. You choose. Go! 1, 2, 3 and stop!

2 Again, and keep to my timing. In to the centre, 3, 4; stay and clap, 3, 4; chasse out, 3, 4; on the spot, you decide. (Keep repeating.)

Movement Skills Training
15 minutes

1 Still in our circle, face anti-clockwise for the circus parade start to what will be our dance. We parade through town, waving to attract the attention of the townspeople.

2 Within the parade, do one action only, and keep repeating it. Front group, be the band with big drumming or blowing actions. Middle group, juggle with really big arm swings. Those at the back, be clowns with silly walks and throwing pails of water.

3 Well done, paraders. Your big actions were eyecatching. Stand in your sixes now, in the positions where I said you would perform. Each group in turn will work by itself in its own circus ring. All the others gather around the performers quickly to watch them and to react to the skill, fun, excitement or danger. Move fast from ring to ring, spectators, as the performers change.

4 Trapezists, in pairs, swing forwards and back, towards and away from each other, then swing forwards and fly to change trapezes.

5 Clowns, do slapstick, funny walks, punching and missing, and throwing pails of water over the spectators.

6 Jugglers, use a repeating pattern of throwing and catching, for example, in front, to the sides, overhead and up behind the back.

7 Tightrope walkers can balance forwards, forwards, wobble, wobble; balance back, back, wobble, wobble, and keep repeating it.

8 Acrobats, do cartwheels, jumps with a turn, tuck or jack-knife, or work with a partner to hold a clever balance.

9 After all the acts by one group, you can do any action of your choice, including one already done such as the band, or a new one such as lion tamer or strong man or woman.

Dance — Umpteen Rings Circus
10 minutes

Music: *TV Sport* from *Festival of Music* by Central Band of the R.A.F.

40 secs	Parade around town
15 secs	Trapeze group
17 secs	Clowns group
16 secs	Jugglers group
19 secs	Tightrope walkers group
16 secs	Acrobats group
17 secs	All do own choice of action
17 secs	Re-form circle for parade from town, waving 'Goodbye! We'll see you next year.'

Dance

Teaching notes and NC guidance
Development over 4 lessons

Pupils should be taught to:

a **respond to music.** This music is an ideal accompaniment to all parts of the dance: the exuberant march into town; all the larger-than-life, circus-work actions; and the 'See you next year!' waving departure from town.

b **create simple characters and narratives.** We 'create' characters by expressing them through whole-body movements normally associated with them. We have to ask 'What are the actions we picture them performing? Where are these actions performed (for example, trapezists swinging forwards to a high point; swinging back through a low point to a high)? How do they move (for example, acrobats with their firm body tension, and beautifully controlled actions; clowns with their floppy, loose, out of control actions)?'

Pupils should be able to show that they can:

a respond imaginatively to the various challenges. **Part of the dance is spent spectating as each group performs.** When the dance is over, the teacher can ask 'Please tell me which of the groups really used their imagination and caught your interest.'

b **repeat sequences with increasing control and accuracy.** The greatest aid to remembering and repeating a sequence is a helpful rhythm and a repeating pattern of two, three or four actions.

Warm-up Activities

1–2 A good warm-up has an easy, almost instant start, actions that make the class think about their movements, and, to gain their attention, something that requires decision-making by them. This one is so easy that they could start, almost without explanation, with the teacher's accompanying, rhythmic 'Skip to the centre, 3, 4; clap hands, clap hands, 3, 4; chasse out, chasse out for 3, for 4; now an action on the spot!' A quick practice of the action on the spot – gesture; bend and stretch; marching steps, etc, will precede subsequent practices of the whole four-part repeating sequence.

Movement Skills Training

1–2 For the anti-clockwise, circling around parade into town, there is a mixture of waving to catch the attention of the townspeople, and a demonstrating of some of the acts to be enjoyed – the band's drumming or trombone blowing; the clever juggling, arm swinging; and the unexpected clowning and water throwing.

3–8 Groups of six are chosen and given their places for their performances. To ensure variety, the teacher decides the action for each group to plan and practise. As each group performs – trapezists, clowns, jugglers, tight-rope walkers and acrobats – all the other groups have to go to watch, moving quickly from 'ring to ring', and express their feelings of pleasure, surprise, wonder or amusement about the acts. To ensure a group unity of action, there will be much direct teaching and suggesting of what to do by the teacher. There will still be plenty of opportunity to 'respond imaginatively' as clowns, for example, create their own choice of funny walks; tight-rope walkers create their own brands of wobbling; jugglers find unusual spaces around themselves for their throwing and catching.

9 The dance ends with everyone deciding and performing their own circus-work action, including, if they wish, something that had not been included already.

Lesson Plan 11 • 30 minutes
April/May

Theme: *Gestures.*

Warm-up Activities
5 minutes

In much the same way that we paraded, waving, in our 'Circus' dance, I want you to march smartly for eight counts, turn on the spot, march for four counts, then make four quick waves to four different classmates. Do not speak. Let your body gestures speak for you. 'Hello!' 'Hi!' Marching, turning, gesturing, go! March smartly, 3, 4, 5, 6, 7, now turn; turn, 2, 3, 4; wave, 2, 3, 4; march briskly, swing your arms, 5, 6, 7, 8; turn, turn, turn, turn; 'Hello! Hello!', 3, 4; again...

Movement Skills Training
15 minutes

1. Gesturing is like speaking with your body. Big gestures after a 'Goal!' are seen every week on TV. Use your body to tell me that you or your team have just scored a 'Goal!'

2. Try it on the spot: walk into it, bringing your punching arm from behind to high in front, or do an enormous leap up on the spot.

3. Try one in slow motion now, which probably means a long arm-pull from behind with your body rotating into the action.

4. Show me the kind of gesture the goalkeeper might make if poor defending caused the goal. Stamping foot? Clenched fist?

5. Later in the game, the referee refuses all demands by team A for a penalty kick. How will team A and its supporters gesture towards the hated referee? Will they point a finger threateningly? Punch a clenched fist, back and forwards?

6. One team A player is so cheeky towards the referee that he is sent off in disgrace. Show me how the referee and all the team B players might signal 'Off!' to this player who is reluctant to go. Will it be one arm pointing in the direction of the changing rooms? Or a hand on hips, head high, look of disgust?

7. One player, trying to influence the referee, falls down and his or her body is gesturing 'Ooooooh! I'm in pain! I was fouled!' How will our crafty actor do this without saying a word?

8. Show me how players in the other team might make a fool of this player, pretending they are all in pain. Show me your body expressing 'Ooooooh! Aaaaaa! Agony!'

Dance — Gestures
10 minutes

1. Well done, goal scorers, supporters, referees and wounded. You did say and gesture things to me without saying a word.

2. Find a partner. Decide who will be asking a favour by gesturing to say 'Please!' or 'You must!' or 'I need it!' or 'Please! I'm desperate!' or 'Give it to me, or else!'

3. Decide who will be replying by gestures, saying 'No!' or 'Never!' or 'You're wasting my time!' or 'You must be joking!' or 'Go away!'

4. You can pretend to be two friends, or parent and child. It's going to be a one-minute struggle to see who wears out the other person with greater determination. Get started, please.

5. One person can walk away at one point and be pursued and confronted by the other one, pleading. Keep struggling, everyone!

6. Let's look at lots of these gesturing duos, and see who we think are the winners. Look out for any surprising gestures, please.

Dance

Teaching notes and NC guidance
Development over 3 lessons

Pupils should be taught to:

a **adopt the best possible posture and use of the body.** If 'gesturing is like speaking with your body', we must try to be eloquent, whole-hearted and even larger than life in the way we use our spine, arms, shoulders and head movements to 'say' something. The focus is on the whole body.

b **express feelings, moods and ideas.** The game provides opportunities to express, by gesture, feelings of joy, disgust, anger, rejection, pain and sarcasm. The partners' dance allows for expressions of pleading and rejection. Expression of the feeling is always through movement.

c **create simple characters and stories.** Referee, goalkeeper, angry players, fouled players; and friends, parent or child characters, and their stories, are all expressed and identified through their whole body gestures and actions.

Pupils should be able to show that they can make simple judgements about their own and others' performances. Couples can watch couples 'speaking with their bodies' after being asked by the teacher 'Tell me if you think the couple you watch are successful in expressing, through their gestures and body movements, particular feelings or emotions. Tell me, also, please, how the expression might be improved.'

Warm-up Activities

This good-fun, instant, easy start to the lesson needs hardly any introductory explanation. The three-part, a: b: c, repeating pattern is accompanied by the teacher's 'March, 2, 3, 4, 5, 6, ready to turn; turn, turn, 3, 4; wave, wave to four others; march again, march again, 5, 6, 7, 8.'

Movement Skills Training

1–8 'No speaking! Say it with your body's actions' and the use of imagery tells the class what we mean by 'Gestures'. Many, watching a match or TV, will already have gestured to express their pleasure at a team's success. The on-the-spot; travel in to; leaping in to; and slow-motion versions of their gestures add the variety of shapes, use of space and different speeds that we are always trying to use to enhance the quality of our movements. Big, whole-body gestures are encouraged, pretending that we are on a stage and wanting spectators at the back of the theatre to recognise what we are expressing. Different body parts are used to help different forms of expressing. Angry foot stamping and punching with clenched fists; dismissive, aggressive rejecting with disgusted arm swings.

Gestures Dance

1–6 In this 25-second competitive gesturing dance, the pleader and the requester try to out-gesture the other, wear them down, make them give in, and gain that something that they want. 'Do not touch your partner, ever. Keep apart and show me your brilliant ways to really demand or really reject. You can walk away, slowly, showing no interest, looking disinterested, bored, confident, strong, while the other has to chase after you, pleading or even threatening you. Do not kneel down, pleading. That is a sign of weakness and you will be a loser. Please show me your best work to show off, later, to the class in our half-watching-half demonstrations. Your 25-second struggle... go!'

Lesson Plan 12 • 30 minutes
May/June

CD
TRACKS
17+20

Theme: *Traditional folk dance.*

Warm-up Activities
6 minutes

1   Partners are numbered one and two. Number one dances, travelling for eight bars of the music, using their own choice of steps. Number two stays on the spot with small, bouncy steps, claps and gestures in time with the music, and two, watch the action or actions of your partner.

2   Partners, change roles, and new travelling partner two use a different travelling step or steps to those of your partner. Number one, you quietly, easily, move on the spot with upper body and arms moving more than legs. Number one, you also watch your partner's travelling.

3   Partners, decide which of your travelling and on-the-spot actions and movements you like best and then plan how to use them as you both dance on the spot, one metre apart, then travel separately but identically with eight counts for each. Keep repeating your on-the-spot and separate travelling actions.

Teach and Dance — Wrona Gapa (Poland)
18 minutes

Music: *Wrona Gapa*, Society for International Folk Dancing.

Formation: Couples form a circle, facing partners with the boy on the inside of the circle. Inside hands are held.

Figure A
Bar 1   Starting with the outside foot (boy's left, girl's right), take one step in line of dance, anti-clockwise, close inside foot, step on outside foot.

Bar 2   Hop on the outside foot, swinging inside leg across outside leg; swing back in opposite direction, hopping again on outside foot.

Bars 3–4   Repeat the above in the opposite direction, changing hands and starting on outside foot (boy's right, girl's left).

Bars 5–8   Repeat bars 1–4.

Figure B
Bars 1–8   Ballroom hold; eight polka steps clockwise. Dance is repeated. (Ballroom hold: Partners face each other. Boy's right arm is around girl, just below shoulder blade. Boy's left arm is forwards at shoulder height with left hand holding girl's right hand. Girl's left hand is on partner's right shoulder, illustrated.)

Revise a Favourite Dance
6 minutes

'Wrona Gapa' is a most lively and vigorous dance with both partners performing non-stop. The final dance should be contrasting and less vigorous, such as a set dance where dancers are involved for only part of the time, or a gentle dance like 'Gestures'.

Dance

Teaching notes and NC guidance
Development over 3 lessons

Pupils should be taught to:

a **respond readily to instructions.** In particular, when the steps or figures of a new dance are not easy, everyone in the class must listen and respond sensibly. Otherwise, the dance will keep breaking down because of one or two who don't know where they are going, what they should be doing, or what is coming next.

b **be mindful of others.** Being 'mindful of others', in this case, means paying full attention to what is being explained so that you and your partner will be successful. It also means giving your partner a helping hand, if necessary, and trying to control all your movements.

c **perform a number of dances from different times and places.** This 'different place' makes an interesting addition to the class repertoire and is extremely vigorous.

Pupils should be able to show that they can remember and repeat a series of movements performed previously. The ability to repeat, practise, improve, learn and remember previous dances is put to the test when the teacher asks the class 'Please suggest a favourite dance for us to finish with.' This invitation also gives the teacher the opportunity to see which dances they seem to have remembered with pleasure – an essential element.

Warm-up Activities

1–3 Ideally, the partners will agree to use one person's travelling actions, and the other partner's on-the-spot actions.

Teach and Dance Wrona Gapa (Poland)

Figure A

Bar 1 Because the music is so fast, the 'step, close, step' with their outside foot will be short, quick steps.

Bar 2 The 'Hop, swing out; hop, swing in' needs to be practised to help the class understand that the swinging leg (right for boys, left for girls) stays up in the air after the first hop so that it can then go straight into a swing the other way.

Bars 3–4 After the second hop, swing in the anti-clockwise circle, they turn to face clockwise to repeat all of the above, facing clockwise.

Bars 5–8 A repetition of everything up to this point.

Figure B

Bars 1–8 If the 8 quick polka steps are too difficult for the class, they can do a more simple 'Step, hop; step, hop; step, hop; step, hop' turn, facing each other, holding both hands to help balance as they turn.

Revise a Favourite Dance

A list of dances in the class repertoire on a notice board in their classroom, and a reminder that they will be given the opportunity to ask for a different-style end-of-lesson dance, will be helpful and might even lead to a mutually agreed decision before they come to the hall.

CD TRACK 24

Theme: *Creating simple characters.*

Warm-up Activities
5 minutes

1   The chase is an exciting part of crime films. Let me see you dodging away on silent feet. Go!

2   When the drum sounds, freeze! Be still so no-one sees you.

3   Your chaser is nearer now, so tiptoe silently from hiding place to hiding place, from alleyways to crouched behind cars.

4   Now, make a break for it with continual right angle turns into passageways and around street corners.

5   Join all the actions together – the quick, silent dodge; the freeze; the slow, silent, tiptoes travel; and the desperate dash.

Movement Skills Training
15 minutes

1   Find a partner and decide who is the cop and who is the robber. Robber, crouch down low, out of sight of the cop who is standing next to you, with his or her back towards you.

2   Robber, silently and slowly, creep away from the policeman.

3   Copper, look to the left and right, twice, while marching on the spot. You frown because you can feel that something is wrong.

4   Policeman, marching with high knee-lift, turn around, see burglar and point at him or her.

5   Burglar, aware that you have been seen, start to run, in slow motion.

6   Cop, point at the escaping robber, while marching on the spot, then move in pursuit of the baddie, now running fast on the spot.

7   Both agree a pattern of four chases, ending with policeman grabbing the robber with one arm.

8   Burglar, throw a custard pie at the policeman who falls.

9   Policeman, pick up a custard pie and throw it. Burglar, fall.

10   Cops and robbers, agree your final action. For example, two pies, thrown at same time, and both fall; or 'Gotcha!' as baddie is held; or one creeps away while other samples and eats the pie.

11   Freeze in your end positions.

Dance – Cops and Robbers
10 minutes

Music: *Easy Winners* by Scott Joplin from the film *The Sting*.

0 secs	Starting positions. Robber, crouch down with policeman's back towards you, and unaware of you.
15 secs	Burglar, slowly, silently, creep away from the policeman.
25 secs	Cop, look to right, left, right and left, very suspicious.
36 secs	Cop, slow march on the spot, then turn, see and point at the burglar.
59 secs	Burglar, do slow-motion running, then faster on spot.
1 min 20 secs	Policeman, slow walk on the spot, then move towards the burglar, starting the chase.
1 min 40 secs	The chase sequence includes slow motion, or on the spot, or much pointing by the policeman who eventually catches and grabs robber with one hand.
2 mins 10 secs	Burglar, throw a custard pie. Policeman, fall down.
2 mins 20 secs	Policeman, throw a pie. Burglar, fall down.
2 mins 32 secs	Partners, agree final action and freeze in it.

Dance

Teaching notes and NC guidance
Development over 3 lessons

Pupils should be taught to:

a   express feelings, moods and ideas.

b   create simple characters and narratives. As always, when trying to be 'expressive' and 'creative', it helps to have a specific image so that the class can easily understand where they are and what they are trying to do.

Pupils should be able to show that they can practise, improve and refine performance. Questioning by the teacher will help to develop and improve the work. 'What will your starting shape be? Proud, upright, swaggering cop? Curled-up, still robber? How will the robber creep away? How will the suspicious cop move to express suspicion? Will your slow-motion chase be on the spot or moving, and how will you best show its slow motion character?' Performance is also improved by demonstrations, followed by comments from the observers. Such comments can include suggestions for improvement.

Warm-up Activities

1–5   A story idea for a warm-up is unusual, but provides excellent images to help pupils understand what is wanted. The 'dodging away' footwork becomes more real when it is seen as part of a chase. The 'freeze' is done more suddenly when it is seen as a warning. The 'tiptoe' moves from hiding places to new hiding places are probably the most silent, restrained ever, to avoid detection. The anxious 'break for it' escape probably includes excellent changes of direction inspired by pictures in their heads of chase scenes.

Movement Skills Training

1–10   This middle part of the dance is a good example of shared-choice teaching. The teacher plans and decides the actions to be included and the class decide the exact nature of those actions. Leaving the planning for every single move and part of the dance to the class is too much to ask them for. Asking the teacher to choreograph every single action and movement in quite a long story dance is too much to ask of the teacher. Asking the class to decide the exact nature of the robber's 'creep away'; the proud, self-confident marching of the police-man or woman; the fearful, slow motion, anxious escape of the burglar; and the triumphant, excited, on-the-spot pursuit by the police, will produce many excellent, individual, unique responses, worth demonstrating, enjoying and learning from.

Lesson Plan 14 • 30 minutes
July

Theme: *Togetherness.*

CD TRACKS 4 + 18

Warm-up Activities
5 minutes

1   Find a partner. Face each other with one hand joined. Number one will dance in a circle around two who turns on the spot. Eight counts.

2   Number two dances in a circle around one who remains, turning, on the spot, with one hand joined. Eight counts.

3   Partners skip together, nearer hands joined, for six counts, then meet with and stand facing another couple, on counts seven and eight.

4   Two counts to each movement: couples reach in and touch right hands at head height, then lower; left hands in, touch and lower; both hands in, touch and lower; all join hands lightly.

5   Couples separate and start again, hands joined, one on spot, one circling around.

Movement Skills Training
15 minutes

1   Before we make our class machine dance all joined together, let's practise some machine-like ways of moving. Show me pushing down actions, like corks into bottles, on the spot or turning, or moving along an assembly line. Pushing down... go!

2   Are you using one hand at a time, or both at the same time? What sort of sounds will accompany your firm pushing? A sudden blowing out of breath; a grunt; 'poom, poom, poom'?

3   A piston action pushes forwards and back. Try this with arms bending and stretching as if you are turning the wheels of a train. Use both arms, one going forwards as one comes back. What kind of whirring, turning sounds will you use?

4   A grabbing machine lifts something up from a passing assembly line, and places it down somewhere else – maybe tins to be packaged. Show me how this might happen. A body-turn to place it would be interesting. Reach; lift; twist; place. 'Choong! Boomp!'

5   Another kind of grabbing machine can dig down, scoop and throw. Are you throwing to left, right or overhead? 'Scoop! Whoosh!'

6   Try an action and reaction. For example, both arms stretched forwards. One arm is still until the other hand strikes it to turn your body through 90 degrees. Or one hand presses down on your head to make your body bend. Other hand strikes under your seat to rise again.

Dance – Our Class Machine
10 minutes

1   Walk in and out of one another, thinking about your favourite kinds of machine action. When I call 'Stop!' be still.

2   Stop! Be still, like switched-off machines. Daniel, at the centre of the class, please start your machine-like movement, with, I hope, some interesting voice sounds.

3   One by one, starting with those nearest to Chris and the centre, move in to link with the machine that started ahead of you.

4   Please try to make our machine interesting with no two linked actions the same. A contrasting set of voice sounds would also be very welcome.

5   Rest for a moment, everyone, and stay in your positions. Can you possibly improve the whole machine's variety by moving more up and down, around, along a short assembly line – or by a brilliant voice sound accompaniment?

Dance

Teaching notes and NC guidance
Development over 3 lessons

Physical Education should involve pupils in the continuous process of planning, performing and reflecting, with the greatest emphasis on the actual performance. For any teacher interested in reflecting on his or her lesson, there are three important post-lesson questions in terms of the National Curriculum.

1 Did I provide opportunities, and challenge the pupils to plan ahead, thoughtfully? Without such planning, there is no focus or thought behind the participation. 'Can you plan...?'; 'Can you show me...?' and 'Show me how...' are questions used to inspire the specific thinking ahead that justifies our calling the lesson 'educational'.

2 Was the time allocated for performing adequate? Was there an impression that the lesson was a 'scene of busy activity with everyone working almost non-stop'? In their performances, did the pupils display quiet, neat, well-controlled work; vigour and poise with some originality; variety and contrast; and the ability to make it all look 'easy'?

3 Were there moments in the lesson when a demonstration was organised and observers were asked to reflect on 'correctness', quality, the main features, what was liked and worth copying, and any ways in which it might be improved? Because they are time-consuming, demonstrations with follow-up comments should only happen once or twice in the lesson.

Warm-up Activities

1–5 Each of the three different actions – dancing around partner on the spot, one hand joined, and other dancing around partner on the spot, one hand joined; partners dance, side by side, nearer hands joined to face another couple; reaching and lowering hands with the other couple – has eight counts and the teacher's chanting can keep pupils all together. 'One circles, 3, 4, the other circles, 3, 4; travel, travel, side by side, meet and stand, right hands ready; right hands, up for 2, right hands, lower for 2; left hands for 2, lower for 2; hands all joined in circle.'

Movement Skills Training

1–6 The teacher challenges ('Show me pushing down actions'); questions ('What sort of sounds will accompany your firm pushing?'); and teaches directly ('Try pushing forwards and back like a piston. Use both arms, one going forwards as one comes back'). In addition, there will be a continuous sharing of good ideas from quick demonstrations.

Our Class Machine Dance

1–5 After the wide variety of machine actions experienced, practised, developed and enjoyed in the middle part of the lesson – both teacher- and pupil-inspired – they should all have a favourite one to include in the created dance climax of the lesson. They start, well spaced apart, all around the room. Only one, centrally placed Daniel, has a specific starting place. Daniel, with own vocal accompaniment and machine-like movement, starts the class machine. Those nearest to Daniel and centre start their move inwards to link with an adjacent machine. Many vocal sounds and varied, machine-like movements make an exciting climax to the programme.

Games

Introduction To Games

Individual and team games are part of our national heritage and an essential part of the physical education programme. Skills learned during games lend themselves to being practised away from school, alone or with friends or parents, and are the skills most likely to be used in participating in worthwhile physical and social activities long after leaving school – an important, long-term aim of physical education.

Vigorous, whole body activity in the fresh air promotes normal, healthy growth and physical development, stimulating the heart, lungs and big muscle groups, particularly the legs. Games lessons come nearest of all physical education activities to demonstrating what we understand by the expression 'children at play'. Pupils are involved in play-like, exciting, adventurous chasing and dodging as they try to outwit opponents in games and competitive activities. Such close, friendly 'combat' with others can help to compensate for the increasingly isolated, over-protected, self-absorbed nature of much of today's childhood.

All the lessons in this book are planned for the playground where most primary school games teaching now takes place. Precious time spent travelling to a field; the high cost of coach travel; a wet, muddy surface for much of the year; the need for expensive footwear; and a playing surface on which it is difficult to practise the variety of activities and small-sided games we need to offer, have all combined to make the school's own playground the preferred setting for the games programme.

Each rectangular third of the netball court is clearly marked with painted lines that should last for several years. These thirds are an ideal size for the three different games that are the climax of each lesson. It is recommended that schools have a line painted from end line to end line, in a different colour to ensure that the netball court is not affected. The extra line means that each rectangle is sub-divided into two halves. The line can be the centre for games across each third and a useful, definite marking for those games, where, for example, you may want to limit defenders or attackers to their own halves. The line can also be a 'net' for summer term games of short-tennis, quoits or volleyball.

The playground 'classroom' rectangle is essential because it contains the whole class in a limited space within which the teacher can see, and be easily seen and heard by, the whole class, and it prevents accidents by keeping the class well away from potential hazards such as concrete seats, hutted classrooms, fences or walls, all of which should be several metres outside the games rectangle.

Games will appeal to, and be very popular with the majority if: the pupils are always moving; the games are exciting; nobody is left doing nothing; they are fun to play; there is plenty of action; and if rules prevent quarrels, let the game run smoothly, let everyone have a turn, and prevent foul play.

The following monthly lesson plans and accompanying explanatory notes are designed to help teachers and schools with ideas for lessons that progress from month to month, and from year to year. Each lesson is repeated three or four times to allow plenty of time for planning, practising, repeating and improving. The plans also aim to provide a focus for staffroom togetherness and unity of purpose regarding the programme's aims, content, teaching methods, standards, and expectations of levels of achievement.

The Games Lesson Plan for Juniors – 30–45 minutes

All of the lessons that follow are designed for the school playground where most primary school games teaching takes place. Each rectangular third of the netball court is an ideal size for the three different, small-sided games or group practices which are the climax of each lesson.

Warm-up and Footwork Practices (4–6 minutes) start the lesson and aim to get the class quickly into action, and stimulate vigorous leg muscle activity which, in turn, stimulates the heart and lungs. Pupils enjoy practising running, jumping, chasing, dodging, marking, changing speed and direction, side-stepping, swerving and accelerating. Older juniors learn correct stopping and starting so that footwork rules in netball and basketball are understood. 'Faking' by moving head, shoulder or foot to one side, then suddenly moving the opposite way; sprint and change of direction dodges; and offensive and defensive footwork, used in 'one against one' dodges, are all practised.

Skills Practices (8–12 minutes) form the middle part of the lesson with the whole class using the same implement and practising the same skills so that the teaching and coaching applies to everyone. With younger, less experienced pupils, the practices include individual then partner practices of skills they might have performed before. They progress on to co-operative and competitive, partner and small group practices of skills already experienced to make practising more like the games situation.

Invent a Game or Skill Practice (3–5 minutes) provides pupils with the opportunity to plan a practice that further develops the skills featured in the middle part of the lesson, or to invent their own game complete with agreed rules and scoring systems.

Group Practices and Small-sided Games (15–22 minutes) can provide one of the most eagerly anticipated parts of all junior school physical education. They are the climax of the lesson and must be started promptly to allow their full time allocation. One of the three games or activities always includes use of the implement and skills practised in the middle part of the lesson. The three games or group practices take part in the thirds of the netball court. If a second court is available, it can be used for any activity that benefits from a bigger playing pitch. The three sets of implements to be used will have been placed adjacent to, but outside, the enclosed rectangles where they will be used.

The main organisational challenge is explaining and starting this final part of the lesson on the first day of a new series of lessons. At the start of the year, the six mixed teams or groups will have been chosen and given 'Your starting place for games and group activities.' If the teacher explains only one game at a time to the ten about to play it, the remaining twenty will be standing, losing heat and patience, and often becoming noisy and inattentive.

The answer is to have all three groups playing the same game or practice, one of the three to be introduced. Instructions about scoring, the main rules and method of re-starting after a score, will apply to all. The signal 'Start!' applies to everyone. When all three games are being played and are obviously understood, the teacher moves to and teaches one group its planned game or activity. When this group is going well, the teacher moves on to and teaches a second group its planned activity. The teacher then says 'Stop, everyone, and look at each of the two games or activities some of you have not seen yet.' Each new game or activity is demonstrated with an accompanying commentary from the teacher. The three groups then rotate on to their second activity, and finally to their third and last activity.

A Pattern for Teaching a Games Skill or Practice

Excellent lesson 'pace' is expressed in almost non-stop activity with no bad behaviour stoppages and no 'dead spots' caused by queues, over-long explanations or too many time-consuming demonstrations. The teaching of each of the skills combining to make a games lesson determines the quality of the lesson's pace'– a main feature of an excellent physical education lesson.

A typical games lesson with its warm-up and footwork practices, skills practices, and small-sided group practices and games, will have about a dozen skills. Whatever the skill, there is a pattern for teaching it.

1 **Quickly into action**. In a few words, explain the task, and challenge the class to start. 'Can you stand, two big steps apart, and throw and catch the small ball to your partner for a two-handed catch?' If a short demonstration is needed, the teacher can work with a pupil who has been alerted. Class practice should start quickly after the five seconds it took the teacher to make the challenge.

2 **Emphasise the main teaching points, one at a time, while the class is working**. z A well-behaved class does not need to be stopped to listen to the next point. 'Hold both hands forward to show your partner where to aim.' 'Watch the ball into your cupped hands.'

3 **Identify and praise good work, while the class is working**. Comments are heard by all; remind the class of key points; and inspire the praised to even greater effort. 'Well done, Sarah and Daniel. You are throwing and catching at the right height and speed, and watching the ball into your hands.'

4 **Teach for individual improvement while class are working**. 'Liam, hold both hands forward to give Lucy a still target to aim at.' 'Chloe and Ben, stand closer. You are too far apart.'

5 **A demonstration can be used**, briefly, to show good quality or an example of what is required. 'Stop everyone, please, and watch how Ravinder and Michael let their hands "give" as they receive the ball, to stop it bouncing out again.' Less than twelve seconds later, all resume practising, understanding what 'giving hands' means.

6 **Very occasionally, to avoid taking too much activity time, a short demonstration can be followed by comments**. 'Stop and watch Leroy and Emily. Tell me what makes their throwing and catching so smooth and accurate.' The class watch about six throws and three or four comments are invited. For example, 'They are nicely balanced with one foot forward.' 'Their hands are well forward, to take the ball early, then give, smoothly and gently.'

7 **Thanks are given to performers and those making helpful comments**. Further practice takes place with reminders of the good things seen and commented on.

Progressing a Games Lesson over 4 or 5 Lessons

Gymnastic activities and dance lessons can begin at a simple level of performing the actions neatly, because they are natural and easy. The challenge for the teacher and class is then to plan and develop movement sequences that link these natural actions together, and refine them by adding 'movement elements' such as changes of speed, direction, shape and tension.

Developing a games lesson is different from the above because the eventual target is the mastery of the specific games skills included in the lesson. Such skills include:

○ good footwork used in stopping, starting, changing direction, chasing after and dodging away from other players

○ sending, receiving and travelling with a ball in invasion, striking/fielding and net games, and controlling other games implements such as skipping ropes, quoits, rackets, hoops and bean bags

○ inventing games with agreed rules in co-operation with a partner or small group. Fairness, safety, lots of action and an understanding of the need for rules are the intended outcomes

○ playing competitive games as individuals, with partners, and in small-sided games

○ understanding the skills and particular roles of players as they attack and defend in the three types of games.

Often the starting point, practising the new skill, is a problem, because controlling the implement is difficult. Balls, bats, hoops, skipping ropes, rackets, quoits and bean bags behave unpredictably and the teacher has to simplify the planned skills to enable pupils to succeed and progress in subsequent lessons. Reception class pupils, for example, might have to walk beside a partner, handing the bean bag to each other, before progressing to throwing and catching. In a Junior school, 2 versus 1 throwing and catching practice, the teacher can ask the defending pupil in the middle to be passive, with arms down at sides, not aiming to 'steal' the ball that is being passed, and only keeping between the two passing players to make them move sideways and forwards, into a good space to receive the ball.

The varied skills headings listed, fit neatly into both infant and junior games lessons, with their:

○ footwork practices

○ skills practices, which can include 'invent a game'

○ group practices and small-sided games, which can include 'invent a game' and challenges to suggest ways to improve a game with a new rule, other ways to score, or limits on player movement.

Step by step, revising the previous lesson's work, and introducing only one teaching point at a time, the teacher progresses one of the skills of the lesson, for example:

1   Try the slow overhead pull of the rope as it slides along the ground towards you.

2   Can you travel, running over the sliding rope, one foot after the other? Which is your leading leg?

3   On the spot, try a jump and bounce for each turn of the rope. (Slow '1 and, 2 and' skipping action.)

4   Try slow running over the rope. Use a small, turning wrist action with hands out wide at waist height.

5   Skip from space to space. Then show me skipping in each space.

6   On the spot, try the slow double beat and the quicker single beat. Then show me neat, non-stop skipping.

7   Pretend your group is on a stage, all doing your best skipping.

Invasion Games for Juniors – the Excitement of Competition

Outwitting one or more opponents – stages in progressing the level of competition

Stage 1 Offensive footwork practices without a ball – starting, stopping, changing direction, accelerating, sprinting, dodging, pivoting, feinting with head, foot or shoulder.

1 Jog, looking for spaces, when near others. Sprint suddenly when you have lots of room.

2 Run freely and change direction on 'Change!'

3 Practise side steps on to new line, still facing the same way.

Stage 2 Co-operative practices with a partner – dodges, direction changes, side steps, body fakes, changes of speed, and helpful comments from following, encouraging partner.

1 Follow your leader who will try dodges to lose you. Follower comments on the dodging.

2 Follow the leader who suddenly sprints to lose you, by speed and direction changes. Follower comments on which was the more successful – speed or direction changes.

3 Jog, side by side, at same speed. Leader does a sudden sprint to be free for a moment.

4 Partners face each other, one metre apart. Attacking partner progresses forward with small, rapid steps to try to make defender lose the 'in line' position between attacker and target line.

Stage 3 Competitive practices with a partner – gives 'attacking' player practice in checking the success of his or her repertoire of offensive dodges.

1 'Tag' where dodger tries to avoid being touched by chaser, who then becomes the dodger.

2 Dodge and Mark. Marker tries to stay within touching distance of dodger on teacher's 'Stop!'

3 One against one, across court, using body feints, plus direction and speed changes.

Stage 4 Offensive footwork practices with a partner, using a ball – trying to reach goal line with ball still in possession in dribbling games such as hockey, football or basketball. These little games need only a short stretch of line as a 'goal' with a 5 metre approach to this line.

1 Teacher allocates a number of minutes for each to attack from a start position 5 metres back. An attack ends when goal is scored, defender takes possession, or ball goes out of area.

2 In '3 lives' games, the same attacker starts three times, then changes roles.

Stage 5 Two against two practices with a ball – two kinds.
1 '3 lives', with same pair attacking three times from a 5 metre approach. After the three turns as attackers are used up, attackers become defenders.

2 End-to-end games across a third of the court with both teams trying to score. Passive defending, with the defending pair marking and keeping 'in line', but not tackling, encourages a flowing, enjoyable game for the less experienced.

Stage 6 Playing 3-, 4- or 5-a-side games – including scaled-down netball, hockey, basketball, football, handball, rugby touch, and created games such as heading ball, skittleball and hoop ball.

1 Attackers ideally understand – 'Pass and move!' 'Give and go to be available!'

2 A named team-mate moves to opponents' line as 'target player' to receive or give passes.

3 'Fast break' every time your team steals possession when none of your team is marked.

National Curriculum Requirements for Games –
Key Stage 2: the Main Features

'The Government believes that two hours of physical activity a week, including the National Curriculum for Physical Education and extra-curricular activities, should be an aspiration for all schools. This applies to all key stages.'

Programme of study Pupils should be taught to:

a play and make up small-sided and modified competitive net, striking/fielding and invasion games

b use skills and tactics and apply basic principles suitable for attacking and defending

c work with others to organise and keep the games going.

Attainment target Pupils should be able to demonstrate that they can:

a select and use skills, actions and ideas appropriately, applying them with co-ordination and control

b when performing, draw on what they know about tactics and strategy

c compare and comment on skills and ideas used in own work by modifying and refining skills and techniques.

Main NC headings when considering assessment, progression and expectation

Planning – Performing and participating in a thoughtful, well-organised way is the result of good planning, which takes place before and during performance. Subsequent performances will be influenced by the planning that also takes place after reflecting on the success or otherwise of the activity. Where planning standards are considered to be satisfactory, there is evidence of: (a) thinking ahead; (b) good judgements and decisions; (c) good understanding; (d) originality; (e) consideration for others; (f) positive qualities such as enthusiasm, whole-heartedness and the capacity for working and practising hard to achieve.

Performing and improving performance – We are fortunate in Physical Education because of the visual nature of the activities. It is easy to see, note and remember how pupils perform, demonstrating skill and versatility. Where standards of performing are satisfactory there is evidence of: (a) neatness, accuracy and 'correctness'; (b) skilfulness and versatility; (c) the ability to remember and repeat; (d) safe, successful outcomes; (e) originality of solutions; (f) ability to do more than one thing at a time, linking a series of actions with increasing fluency, accuracy, control and skill; (g) ability to make sudden adjustments as needed; (h) pleasure from participation; (i) a clear understanding of what was required.

Evaluating/reflecting – Evaluation is intended to inform further planning and preparation by helping both performers and spectators with guidance and ideas for altering, adapting, extending and improving performances. Where standards in evaluating are satisfactory, pupils are able to: (a) observe accurately; (b) identify the parts of a performance that they liked; (c) pick out the main features being demonstrated; (d) make comparisons between two performances; (e) reflect on the accuracy of the work; (f) comment on the quality of the movement, using simple terms; (g) suggest ways in which the work might be improved; (h) express pleasure in a performance.

Year 4 Games Programme

Pupils should be able to:

Autumn	Spring	Summer
1 Respond readily to instructions and signals and follow sensible rules of behaviour.	1 Use vigorous leg action to keep warm on cold days and to develop heart, lungs and fitness.	1 Revise, practise and refine skills of net and striking/ fielding games, by yourself and with others.
2 Recognise the need for safety considerations in dress and sharing of space.	2 Develop versatility in passing a ball at different heights and speeds to outwit a close-marking opponent, sometimes using a 'fake'.	2 Show ability to sustain energetic activity.
3 Repeat and improve skills learned previously, showing confidence and control.		3 Send a ball longer distances with an overarm throw.
4 Start to anticipate direction of passes and try to intercept.	3 Lead and follow a partner to practise quick responses and to practise observing movement.	4 Bowl underarm with confidence and accuracy, understanding 'good length'.
5 Demonstrate neat, quiet running.	4 Play fairly, compete honestly and demonstrate good sporting attitudes and behaviour.	5 Apply attacking principles of hitting into space, varying direction and judging when and if to run.
6 Revise good dodging and marking footwork with quick stops and starts, changes of speed and direction, and 'fake' moves.	5 Demonstrate the ability to plan and refine a performance to achieve greater efficiency.	6 Back one another up as fielders.
7 Start to mark a player, with and without the ball, and cover defensive team-mates.	6 Plan and play own versions of recognised team games, sometimes restricting attackers and defenders to keep the game open with more space for passing a ball.	7 Plan and create your own versions of recognised games, deciding rules to keep games moving with all involved.
8 Practise a variety of ways to send, receive and carry a ball – throw, catch, head, kick, bounce, dribble, volley.		8 Plan and use simple tactics in a range of games and judge their effectiveness.
9 Learn to 'give and go'; 'Pass and follow'; 'Run to a space if you want to receive a pass', constantly planning ahead.	7 Plan, use and be able to explain simple tactics to outwit an opponent.	9 Enjoy the variety of games able to be played in warmer weather – invasion, net and striking/ fielding.
10 Demonstrate an understanding of simple skills and principles in attack and defence in invasion games, e.g. 'one-on-one' marking 'in line' in defence.	8 Include '3 lives' games to concentrate on one thing at a time – attack or defence.	10 Explore and understand common skills and principles in games – side towards ball when striking; preparatory back swing before hitting; moving early to be in position to receive.
	9 Use a 'fast break' on gaining possession to outrun the opponents to their goal line.	11 Plan decisions thoughtfully.
	10 Make simple, helpful comments and judgements on others' performances.	

Year 4

Lesson Plan 1 • 30-45 minutes
September

Warm-up and Footwork Practices
4—6 minutes

1 Run freely, using the whole area, keeping clear of others and not following anyone. When I call 'Stop!' be in a space by yourself. Stop! (Repeat.)

2 All-against-all tag, using two thirds of netball court. Count the number that you tag and count how often you are tagged.

Skills Practices: with Small Balls
8—12 minutes

Individual practices

1 Walk or jog slowly, throwing and catching with both hands at eye level.

2 Can you walk forwards bouncing the ball on to the ground with the fingertips of one hand? Have a try with right and left hands.

Partner practices

1 Throw for your partner to catch, standing 3 metres apart. Receiving partner should have hands forwards as a target.

2 Can you show me other ways in which you can send the ball to your partner, standing or on the move?

Invent a Game or Games Practice in 2s
3—5 minutes

Can you invent a throwing and catching practice or game where one partner remains on the spot while the other partner moves? (For example, player with ball counts his throws and catches while partner races to touch a line and come back to starting place next to partner. Change over and see who made more catches.)

Group Practices and Small-sided Games
15—22 minutes

Small ball each

Practise many ways of throwing and catching. One hand to same, one to opposite, 1 to 2, 2 to 1, at different heights, still and on the move.

Bench-ball

Pass to team-mate on bench to score. Change bench-catcher often, particularly in cold weather. Decide on your main rule and how to re-start after a goal.

Skipping rope each

With feet together, can you skip forwards, backwards and sideways? Now can you travel forwards, skipping with a walking or running action (illustrated)?

Games

Teaching notes and NC guidance
Development over 4–5 lessons

Lesson's main emphases:

a The NC general requirements to respond readily to instructions, be physically active and work safely, alone and with others.

b Pupil co-operation to enable the lesson to flow, almost non-stop, from running start to 3 groups ending, to give enough time for each of the 3 groups, which is the climax and main part of the lesson. 'Dead spots', when nothing is happening because of noise, slow responses or bad behaviour, should not be tolerated.

Equipment: 30 small balls; 1 large ball; 10 skipping ropes.

Warm-up and Footwork Practices

1 Emphasise that the first running practice is to re-establish space awareness in the class, while moving about within the netball court playground 'classroom'. The year's Games programme starts with lively action, concerned with safety and immediate responses, setting the standard for all future lessons.

2 In the tag game, emphasise 'Touch gently to catch someone. No hard, dangerous pushing which could lead to broken bones.'

Skills Practices: with Small Balls

Individual practices

1 Let the arms recoil on catching with fingers folding around the ball. They should be looking closely at the ball throughout.

2 In bouncing, use wrist action with no movement in elbow or shoulder. A slight bending in the knees helps the dribbler to be down nearer the ball and in better control of it.

Partner practices

1 With a partner, show thrower where you want the ball by holding hands forwards at upper-chest height for a throw you can see and catch easily. Throw is helped by a preliminary swing back of the throwing arm, then the reach forwards and aiming throw.

2 Other ways to send? Kick, head, bat, roll, bounce, side by side throwing, rugby style, with both hands.

Invent a Game or Games Practice in 2s

If the class is unused to inventing a game, give them one to try until they become used to this short part of the lesson, where we want them to become more thoughtful, independent and appreciative of the necessity for rules, fairness and sharing.

Group Practices and Small-sided Games

Small ball each

September is still warm enough, usually, for a last practice of small-ball skills that are associated with summer's fielding/striking games.

Bench-ball

In bench-ball, only the bench-catcher is allowed to stand on the rectangular 'bench', marked with chalk. 4 or 5 a side play in one third of the netball court.

Skipping rope each

Skipping, when kept going, is excellent for 'sustaining energetic activity' and is a first-class leg muscles exercise.

Lesson Plan 2 • 30-45 minutes
October

Warm-up and Footwork Practices
4–6 minutes

1 Run quietly and try to feel a lifting in your heels, knees, arms, chest and head.

2 10-points tag. All have 10 points to start with. Lose 1 point every time you are tagged.

Skills practices: with large balls
8–12 minutes

Individual practices

1 Can you throw the ball above your head a short distance, jump and catch at full stretch, and land well balanced?

2 Dribble by hand using fingertips. Try left and right hands.

Partner practices

1 Throw above partner's head for a stretched jump and catch above head.

2 Pass to partner, 3 metres away; 2-handed chest pass; move sideways and forwards to a new space to receive pass from partner. Receive, pass, move, receive.

Invent a Game or Games Practice in 2s
3–5 minutes

Using part of a line as a target or goal, can you invent a game that involves sending the ball towards it in some way?

Group Practices and Small-sided Games
15–22 minutes

Large ball between 2
Practise freely sending the ball to your partner on the spot or moving, e.g. throw and catch, kick, head, volley, running rugby fashion, etc.

Skittle-ball, with 2 target skittles in each hoop
Score by knocking skittle down. No-one may stand inside the hoop.

Team passing large ball
2 v 1 or 2 v 2 where 3 good passes to team-mate equal 1 goal (illustrated). Encourage 'pass and run to a new space', 'short passes at about 3 metres', and include bounce, 2-handed, chest and 1-handed shoulder passes.

Games

Teaching notes and NC guidance
Development over 4–5 lessons

Lesson's main emphases:

a The NC requirements to improve the skills of sending, receiving and travelling with a ball, to make appropriate decisions quickly and to plan responses.

b Much running in the warm-up, the skills practices and in all three games. We also run smartly to each new part of the lesson, responding quickly to commands to save time and to keep warm.

Equipment: 30 large balls; 2 hoops; 4 skittles.

Warm-up and Footwork Practices

1 The 'run quietly' start needs an explanation. 'Feel your heels, knees, arms, chest and head lifting.'

2 In 10-points tag, emphasise that you touch 'gently, with no hard pushing lest someone falls and breaks a bone.' Stop game every 12 seconds to maintain control, calm pupils down, and to check on 'who are the best dodgers, caught only 2 or 3 times? Which best catchers caught 5 or more?'

Skills practices: with large balls

Individual practices

1 Much linking of skills into 'increasingly complex sequences' here with the throw, jump to catch, and balanced landing.

2 In dribbling by left or right hand, the challenge to develop is 'can you change the speed, direction and height of your dribble?'

Partner practices

1 Partners stand next to each other for the vertical throw up for a jump up to catch at full height and stretch, before landing well balanced on both feet. Catching partner should wait until ball starts to descend, then spring up to meet it.

2 A pass to partner and run to space to receive pass can be expanded by adding a fake pass before the real thing.

Invent a Game or Games Practice in 2s

Sending by reckless, hard kicking is the least satisfactory method, and usually someone has to be stopped from doing it. Send by heading, batting, bouncing, easy throwing after a fake, or even by dribbling over the line by hand or foot.

Group Practices and Small-sided Games

Large ball between 2

Send the ball 3 metres to your partner to allow easy receiving and lots of repetitions. Send in front of a travelling partner when side by side. Send into the space ahead of a partner who is facing you and moving sideways.

Skittle-ball

In skittle-ball, 'Pass and run forwards to help. Run into a space if you want to be passed to; don't stand, shouting for it.' A diamond-shape attack is good for advancing the ball. One at rear keeps an eye on own goal. One well ahead is target person. 2 in mid-court advance ball and themselves.

Team passing large ball

Stop the '2s' from standing miles apart and throwing over the heads of the others. Insist on '3-metres-apart passing'.

Lesson Plan 3 • 30-45 minutes
November

Warm-up and Footwork Practices
4—6 minutes

1   Run well and quietly without following anyone. Show me slow running when near others or in a corner, and sprint running when there is plenty of space.

2   Tag, where 6 chasers can touch you if you are running about within the lines. You can 'hide' or take refuge on the lines. When caught, take a band and help the chasers.

Skills Practices: with hockey sticks and balls
8—12 minutes

Individual practices

1   Run, with right hand carrying stick in the middle like a suitcase, flat side to left and head of stick forwards.

2   On 'Change!' place left hand at the top of your stick, leaving right hand where it is. Carry in front, head of stick near ground, ready to receive ball.

3   Run with stick in both hands with its head almost touching ground and in front of you. Flat side is forwards and slightly to the right. Gently push ball ahead of you with many little touches, feeling how easy it is to send ball forwards.

Invent a Practice
3—5 minutes

Can you invent a practice, travelling with the ball, using the lines in some way. (Consider using direction changes, zigzags, etc.)

Group Practices and Small-sided Games
15—22 minutes

Hockey stick and ball each

Walk around with ball glued to stick. Can you jog or run? Now run around, ball glued to stick and trying to turn little circles. Emphasise stick in constant contact with ball and angled to the ground.

Mini-basketball, netball apparatus

Netball apparatus in 3 metres from end so that ball is not continually going out of court. Encourage 'pass and move' to advance ball, but basketball dribbling allowed. 1 point for near miss, hitting hoop, 2 points when ball goes through ring.

Large ball between 2

Hand, foot and heading tennis, sending ball to partner over chalk line 'net' (illustrated). How long a rally can you make? Invent a simple 1 v 1 game with one main, fair rule.

Games

Teaching notes and NC guidance
Development over 4–5 lessons

Lesson's main emphases:

a The NC requirements to sustain energetic activity, understand what happens to our bodies during exercise, and plan, perform and reflect on their own games and practices.

b Becoming and staying warm by doing all the activities 'on the move'. Using our legs so strongly and continuously warms us up easily and we know that only wet weather will stop us going outside to enjoy our lively, varied and exciting Games lessons.

Equipment: 30 hockey sticks and small balls; 6 large balls.

Warm-up and Footwork Practices

1 Running along straight lines so as not to follow others should now be a feature of the class running. In the anti-clockwise, curving running seen in many primary schools, all follow each other.

2 If anyone is non-adventurous in tag, lingering on the lines to avoid being caught, the teacher must call out 'All move!' at regular 5-second intervals.

Skills Practices: with hockey sticks and balls

Individual practices

1 The controlled carry of the stick by the right side prevents dangerous swinging of the stick and easily transfers to the push position with both hands in front of you.

2 On 'Change!' the change to a push stroke hold in front is immediate and neat.

3 Emphasise how dangerous a hockey stick can be if swung wildly behind or in front of you. Stick is placed behind ball which is pushed away carefully. There is no noise of stick hitting ball and no backswing as a preparation for a hit.

Invent a Practice

Pupils can be asked to 'feel' how the stick is held firmly by the left hand and allowed to rotate in the looser grip of the right hand. This allows rotation of the head of the stick to move the ball from side to side or forwards and back.

Group Practices and Small-sided Games

Hockey stick and ball each

Beanbags or skittles spread around the third of the netball court provide obstacles to dribble around. Teacher can check control by calling 'Stop!' to see how quickly pupils can bring ball to a standstill using the stick.

Mini-basketball, netball apparatus

In mini-basketball, dribbling by hand is allowed. However, passing is always a quicker way to advance the ball, and dribbling should be discouraged when a team-mate is in a space, free to receive a pass. Encourage lots of shooting by awarding 1 point for a near miss, when the ball hits the ring but does not go through the hoop.

Large ball between 2

Playing across a third of the netball court gives lots of little courts for 1 versus 1 games over chalk line drawn as a 'net'. Use hand, foot or head, or, by agreement, a combination, for an enjoyable game where good rallies are possible. Decide how many points in a game – 5 is a good number – then change ends.

Year 4

Lesson Plan 4 • 30–45 minutes
December

Warm-up and Footwork Practices
4–6 minutes

1. Run, emphasising good 'straight-ahead' position of head, shoulders, arms and legs.

2. Dodge and mark in 2s. Marker chases dodger. On command 'Stop!' see who is the winner – dodger who can't be touched by partner, or marker who can still reach to touch dodging partner. Change duties and repeat.

Skills Practices: with rugby or large balls
8–12 minutes

Individual practices

1. Run, carrying ball in both hands in front of you, letting it swing naturally from side to side.

2. Throw ball above head height a short distance; jump to catch it at full stretch; grab it in to your chest with both hands.

Partner practices

Jog side by side, passing ball just in front of partner for easy, two-handed catch (illustrated). Change sides often to practise passing to both left and right.

Invent a Skills Practice in 2s
3–5 minutes

Invent a simple chasing and dodging game with 1 rugby ball between 2 players (e.g. one with ball chases after partner to try to touch him on hips with ball held in both hands).

Group Practices and Small-sided Games
15–22 minutes

Rugby-touch

When touched, release ball or pass to team-mate. Score when ball is placed on ground behind opponents' end line. Think of ways to increase scoring chances (e.g. have a catcher on line).

Ground-football

Score by arriving on opponents' end line with ball under control under foot, or pass to team-mate near end line. Encourage 'pass often, dribble seldom.'

2 v 2 hockey across half pitch

You score by placing ball on opponents' goal line. Push pass: stick on ground behind ball and push with strong, right hand action.

Games

Teaching notes and NC guidance
Development over 4–5 lessons

Lesson's main emphases:

a   The NC requirements to understand and play small-sided versions of recognised games, to work vigorously to develop suppleness, strength and stamina, and to exercise the heart and lungs strongly.

b   Being guided by those children who, when asked to comment, say that a Games lesson appeals to them when 'it is fun to play; is always going; is exciting; no-one is left doing nothing; there is lots of action; the rules prevent quarrels, let the game run smoothly, let all have a turn and prevent rough, foul play.'

Equipment: 30 large or rugby balls; 1 large or medium flattish round ball; 10 hockey sticks and 2 small balls.

Warm-up and Footwork Practices

1   'Straight-ahead' running practice to make children aware of their arms, shoulders and feet, parts which often deviate from the straight ahead and twist inefficiently from side to side.

2   On command 'Stop!' insist on an instant stop to check winner. If either player takes one step after game is stopped, the wrong result happens. Insist on good dodging, not fast sprinting away.

Skills practices: with rugby or large balls

Individual practices

1   Only in rugby games are we allowed to run carrying the ball. Practise the run and carry, with hands spread around the ball and arms swinging easily from side to side.

2   The 'grab in' to chest with both hands is a good habit to practise in a game where possession is everything.

Partner practices

Partner passing is often described as 'sympathetic' by rugby coaches, meaning that passer's aim and force must be just right and just ahead of partner for an easy, well-placed and well-timed catch.

Invent a Skills Practice in 2s

If trying the 1 versus 1 game suggested, insist on a very small area to help chaser. They could play end-to-end rugby-touch across part of a third of the netball court. When touched, ball must be put on ground for opponent.

Group Practices and Small-sided Games

Rugby-touch

The touching of an opponent in rugby-touch must be gentle. 'No hard pushing allowed. It's dangerous.' Ask catchers to try to take the pass near to the passer and on the move to advance quickly.

Ground-football

Ground-football with a softish ball that does not roll away. Some limits on the defenders will produce a calmer game. A 'no tackling' rule is a suggestion to give attackers more confidence.

2 v 2 hockey across half pitch

2 versus 2, half-pitch hockey needs an agreed main rule and some limits on the defenders to help game flow. Such limits might include defenders being 'passive' and not allowed to tackle.

Lesson Plan 5 • 30-45 minutes
January

Warm-up and Footwork Practices
4—6 minutes

1   Run freely over whole netball court. To avoid others coming towards you, use a little side-step: one foot goes straight to the side, putting you on a new line but in the same direction.

2   Chain-tag. 3 or 4 couples start as chasers, When caught, join the chain that tagged you, When 4 in chain, split into 2 pairs and continue chasing. Last caught wins.

Skills Practices: with large balls
8—12 minutes

Individual practices

1   Dribble using different surfaces of both feet, keeping ball close.

2   Gently toss ball up to hit you on the head, then catch it. Use forehead and keep eyes open.

Partner practices

Shadow dribbling, 1 ball between 2, front person dribbling, other following behind. Change over after 6 touches.

Invent a Game or Skills Practice in 2s
3—5 minutes

Can you invent a simple game with a part of a line, 1 ball between 2? (for example, heading to see how many consecutive headers; throw up to self to head past partner on line.)

Group Practices and Small-sided Games
15—22 minutes

1 large ball among 4

3 v 1 where '1' tries to win ball from 3 players who are inter-passing, football fashion. Decide a rule to give '1' a fair chance to win ball.

Heading-ball

Foam ball, 4 or 5 a side. Score by heading pass from team-mate over the opponents' end line. (N.B. 2 people must be involved in every goal.)

Change-bench-ball, 4 or 5 a side

One passes to team-mate on chalk bench to score, then changes places with him.

Games

Teaching notes and NC guidance
Development over 4–5 lessons

Lesson's main emphases:

a The NC requirements to explore and understand the common skills and principles, including attack and defence, in invasion games, and to play fairly, compete honestly and demonstrate good sporting behaviour.

b 'What you don't use, you lose.' In this lesson we are vigorously using the legs throughout. By exercising legs and heart muscle so strongly, we develop their strength and assist in their normal, desirable growth.

Equipment: 30 large balls; 1 large foam ball.

Warm-up and Footwork Practices

1 In the side-step there is no direction change, just a change of line to a parallel one.

2 In chain-tag, emphasise 'Gentle touch to catch someone. No hard pushing or shoving.' Dodgers are encouraged to use good dodges such as direction and speed changes, and head, foot and shoulder fakes, rather than high-speed running away.

Skills Practices: with large balls

Individual practices

1 In football dribbling, test class with an occasional 'Stop!' to see how quickly they bring ball under foot, still and under control.

2 In heading, feel the upper body and legs being active and coming into the action so that the ball is struck firmly by the forehead.

Partner practices

Shadow dribbling tests the dribbler's ability to repeat a short sequence, and tests the following observer's ability to recognise and copy the actions exactly.

Invent a Game or Skills Practice in 2s

Games involving travelling with the ball to take it just over the line to score have the advantage that the ball is not continually wandering away, as when you score by sending it across the line.

Group Practices and Small-sided Games

1 large ball among 4

In 3 versus 1, passing and screening, football fashion, a large flattish ball is recommended because it is easier to keep it in the limited area. For example, allow the passers 1 touch only before they have to pass, to give the '1' a chance.

Heading-ball

A target player on opponents' line can head a pass made, or catch and pass back to a running team-mate who shoots.

Change-bench-ball

Player leaving chalk 'bench' should pass to a team-mate on court, then leave bench to make way for the one who made the scoring throw to come on to bench. A game of quick reactions. Keep awake!

Lesson Plan 6 • 30-45 minutes
February

Warm-up and Footwork Practices
5–7 minutes

1   Run beside partner, keeping together at same speed.

2   Now A changes speed over a very short distance to lose B in a sprint dodge. Change over dodgers.

3   Couples-tag. 3 couples start as chasers. When one of the pair touches a dodger, the caught dodger changes place with the chaser who touched him to form a new chasing couple.

Skills Practices: with hockey sticks and balls
7–10 minutes

Individual practices

1   Walk with ball 'glued' to open side of stick. When you see a space about 2–3 metres ahead, push pass the ball into this space. Run after ball and repeat.

2   Indian dribble (turning stick up and down). Hold flat side of stick against ball with stick head pointing up, to right of ball. Now point head down and transfer to other, left-hand side of ball. Move ball left and right with stick head pointing up and down.

3   Walk, moving ball from left to right to left in a curving formation around beanbags, cones, quoits, etc.

Invent a Hockey Practice in 2s
3–5 minutes

Can you invent a simple practice that we might all enjoy that keeps you both moving and uses and improves dribbling and pushing?

Group Practices and Small-sided Games
15–23 minutes

Hockey games, half pitch

2 v 2, 3 'lives'. Attackers score by push passing ball through goal, and have 3 lives. When they lose possession 3 times, attackers become defenders.

Free-netball

4 or 5 a side. No limitations on who can score or where you can go. No dribbling. To advance ball, run forwards into space, particularly after passing.

Handball

4 or 5 a side. Goal scored when ball thrown between posts from outside 6-metre shooting circle. Decide rule to keep game moving, e.g. you must shoot after 3 passes.

Games

Teaching notes and NC guidance
Development over 4–5 lessons

Lesson's main emphases:

a The NC requirements to improve the skills of sending, receiving and travelling with a ball, and to play small-sided versions of recognised games.

b Recognising that vigorous physical exercise, particularly in the fresh air, makes you fitter, is good for your heart, and makes you look and feel better. In winter, when we spend most of our time indoors, these lessons become even more important for young, growing children.

Equipment: 30 hockey sticks and small balls; 2 large balls.

Warm-up and Footwork Practices

1 Partner side-by-side running is an exercise in co-operation to maintain a steady, unchanging running rhythm together.

2 The sprint-dodge practice shows the partners how easily a sudden, unexpected sprint can lose an opponent, to free the sprinter, for example, to receive a pass or shoot.

3 Encourage the dodgers to use good footwork rather than high-speed running away to evade chasers. Direction changes, sprint dodges, and head and shoulder fakes should all be tried. Ask the 3 or 4 starting chasing couples to space themselves out over the thirds of the netball court.

Skills Practices: with hockey sticks and balls

Individual practices

1 In dribbling, the ball is in front of you, being pushed ahead by a series of gentle taps. To give ball a gentle push ahead, turn body slightly to face right, place stick behind ball, now between feet, and push without a sound as ball is hit.

2 In Indian zigzag dribbling, emphasise the dominance of the upper left hand in turning stick, and the sleeve-like right hand allowing ball to rotate both ways.

3 Use this left-hand turning of the stick to dribble the ball up to, in between and around the scattered obstacles.

Invent a Hockey Practice in 2s

For example, partners stand about 10 metres apart, one on a side line, other ready with ball. One with ball responds to signals of watching partner as he advances to partner's line. Agree a set of signals: dribble straight; dribble zigzag; push ahead a short distance; push to me.

Group Practices and Small-sided Games

Hockey games, half pitch

Half pitch, '3 lives' games allow both defenders and attackers to concentrate on one thing at a time. Teams should agree one main rule, how to re-start and how to limit opponents.

Free-netball

In free-netball, encourage shooting by giving 1 point for a near miss when ball hits hoop but does not go through. Some limit on where defenders and attackers may go will open up the game.

Handball

Aim for 'fast break' to opponents' end when your team gains possession, and have a target player to whom to try and pass.

Year 4

Lesson Plan 7 • 30-45 minutes
March

Warm-up and Footwork Practices
4—6 minutes

1   Run, jump, land in 2 counts. Count '1' is back foot, which must not move. With heel of back foot up and toes into ground, turn around or pivot other foot on '2'. Let front foot find a space. Repeat.

2   Free-and-caught. If caught by 1 of the 6 chasers in coloured bands, stand still, with hands on top of head. Others can free you by touching your elbows. Change chasers frequently.

Skills Practices: with rugby balls or large balls
6—8 minutes

Partner practices

1   All pairs in a third of netball court. Try to make a short pass of 2–3 metres, rugby fashion, to your partner. Pass at varied heights and speeds to avoid others around you, and according to the situation.

2   Shuttle pick-up-and-place in 4s. A picks up ball from hoop, runs to put it in opposite hoop and stays at back of opposite line. B repeats to other side, and so on.

Develop a Whole-class Game where Half have a Ball
4—6 minutes

If touched by one without ball, put yours down for another to pick up. What other rules could develop this game? (For example, ball-carrier may touch another with ball then have 2 rugby balls if quick enough to pick up his when placed on ground.)

Group Practices and Small-sided Games
16—25 minutes

Rugby-touch

4 or 5 a side. Score by placing ball behind opponents' end line (illustrated). If touched you must pass ball. After score, opponents throw ball from behind their goal line. Stress 'Run forwards to gain ground until touched.'

Ground-football

4 or 5 a side; large, flattish ball. Keep ball below knee height at all times. Score by placing foot on ball on opponents' goal line. Stress 'Receive ball, look for team-mate in a space, pass, then follow to help.'

Playground-hockey

4 or 5 a side. Score by placing stick on ball on opponents' goal line. For more open game, tell left and right side forwards or defenders to stay on their own sides of the court.

Games

Teaching notes and NC guidance
Development over 4–5 lessons

Lesson's main emphases:

a The NC requirement to work safely, alone and with others, and to plan, perform and reflect.

b A strong sense of 'togetherness' within the class from the group chasing game; skills practices with a partner, then in lines of 4; a whole class chasing and dodging game where we are invited to invent some developments; and finally 3 small-sided versions of popular games where we feel strongly the sense of being in a team.

Equipment: 15 rugby or large balls; 1 flattish large ball; 10 hockey sticks and 1 playground hockey ball.

Warm-up and Footwork Practices

1 A 2-count stop when receiving ball on the move applies in netball and in basketball. The front foot, which landed second, may be moved to let you see around you or to take you and ball away from a defender. This action on a still rear foot is called 'pivoting'.

2 In free-and-caught, ask the 6 chasers to space out, with 2 covering each third of the netball court. Have more chasers if the 'freers' keep winning easily.

Skills Practices: with rugby balls or large balls

Partner practices

1 All of class in a third of the court, trying to interpass in 2s, requires much care, self-control and a good awareness of all around you. In rugby, you are allowed to run with the ball, which helps because you have more time.

2 Shuttle pick-up from, or run and score in, a hoop. This is a sprint pick-up-and-score practice, involving one player at a time only.

Develop a Whole Class Game where Half have a Ball

In a lesson with a high level of social activity, a whole class 'invents and develops a game started and suggested by the teacher'. This should provide some good ideas, fun and excitement.

Group Practices and Small-sided Games

Rugby-touch

In rugby-touch, insist on gentle touching and no hard, dangerous pushing. With a good class, we can say 'no forwards passing allowed in the opponents' half, but you may pass forwards to advance ball to the halfway line.'

Ground-football

Ground-football needs 1 rule to help keep game open, by limiting attackers or defenders in some way. For example, '2 touches only in attack. Defenders may shadow, but must not tackle.'

Playground-hockey

Restrictions on defenders and attackers, as suggested, aim to keep game open with all spaced out better with more room to pass.

Lesson Plan 8 • 30-45 minutes
April

Year 4

Warm-up and Footwork Practices
4—6 minutes

1   Follow your leader. Can you include some hurdling across the lines and some scissor jumps with nearer leg swinging up and over the line?

2   Cross-court sprint relays in 2s, starting side by side at centre of court. One races to side line and back to touch partner, who races to touch his side line and sprints back. Make 8 touches each. Go!

Skills Practices: with bats and balls and skipping ropes
8—12 minutes

Individual practices

Bat and ball
1   Walk, striking ball up, letting it bounce, striking it up.

2   Walk, batting ball down on to ground, making it rise to waist height.

Ropes
1   Skip on the move with feet together or one after the other.

2   Can you skip, travelling forwards, backward and sideways?

Partner practices

Bat and ball
1   3 metres apart, one throws with gentle bounce for partner to strike back.

2   A strikes with own hand to B who catches at various heights.

Ropes
1   Can you follow your leader and build up to mirroring each other in your actions?

2   1 rope between 2. Show me ways in which 2 can skip (illustrated).

Group Practices and Small-sided Games
18—27 minutes

Skipping rope each with a partner
Show your partner some of your favourite ways to skip.

Non-stop cricket
1 ball and 1 bat among 4 or 5. Batter must run around post after hitting ball. Change duties often.

Mini-basketball with netball posts
4 or 5 a side. For a more open game, ask left and right forwards and guards to keep to own side of court. Score 1 point for near miss and 2 for shot through basket. Decide on rule to keep game moving, e.g. no dribbling in own half. Pass and run forwards to help!

Games

Teaching notes and NC guidance
Development over 4–5 lessons

Lesson's main emphases:

a The NC general requirements to develop skill by exploring and making up activities, and to practise, improve and repeat longer sequences of movement.

b Remembering that our lessons take account of the time of year with very lively lessons in mid-winter, full of almost non-stop, running activities and games to make and keep us warm. This means trying to cover most of the less lively net/ball and striking/fielding practices and games from April onwards.

Equipment: 16 small bat shapes and 16 small balls; 16 skipping ropes; 2 sets wickets or cones; 1 large ball.

Warm-up and Footwork Practices

1–2 Many athletic activities – running, jumping and throwing – are being performed in every Games lesson. We concentrate on their 'athletic-ness' more obviously from April onwards. 'Over, 1, 2, 3, over' in hurdling as we clear the imaginary hurdle on 'over', then take 3 steps between our hurdles on '1, 2, 3'. We help children discover their natural leading leg in hurdling, their swinging-up leg in scissor jumping, and how to sprint off quickly from a semi-crouched start position in the relays.

Skills Practices: with bats and balls and skipping ropes

Bat and ball and skipping practices are done individually then with a partner, with the same equipment, before changing to the other item of equipment for individual then partner practices. The very physical skipping contrasts well with the less vigorous bat and ball practices. Half the class are working with each of the 2 implements typically associated with the warmer weather of spring, summer and early autumn.

Group Practices and Small-sided Games

Skipping rope each with a partner

With good performers, skipping with a partner can progress to 2 skipping with 1 rope, to expand the class repertoire of skipping ideas and to practise 'sustained energetic activity', as required in the NC. Partners alternating to give non-stop skipping is also worth trying.

Non-stop cricket

Non-stop cricket is even more 'non-stop' when good bowling makes the batter hit the ball, which means the batter has got to run. While the batter is running, all are involved in fielding, backing up the wicket or trying to give ball to bowler who bowls, whether or not the batter is at the wicket. Poor bowling, when the batter does not have to hit the ball, means no action for anyone.

Mini-basketball with netball posts

In mini-basketball, where we can apply the 2-count footwork rule met and practised last month, encourage lots of shooting by giving 1 point for a near miss when the ball hits the hoop, and 2 points when the ball goes through the hoop. Bring posts in 2 metres from end line so that a missed shot stays in play.

Year 4

Lesson Plan 9 • 30-45 minutes
May

Warm-up and Footwork Practices
4–6 minutes

1 Stay in one third of the netball court, space out sensibly and find out how many: (a) long hops; (b) bounding steps; and (c) jumps from 2 feet to 2 feet you need to take you across your third from line to line.

2 Now run around the whole netball court, jogging one third, sprinting the middle third, jogging the end third. Turn back and repeat.

Skills Practices: with short-tennis rackets, balls and hoops
8–12 minutes

Individual practices

Racket and ball

1 Walk, bouncing ball up on face of racket.

2 Walk, hitting it up, letting it bounce, hitting it up. Soft hits.

Hoop

1 Show me how you can use the hoop on the ground.

2 What can you do with the hoop, using 1 or 2 hands (illustrated)?

Partner practices

Short tennis

1 One throws gently underarm to partner's forehand. Partner does forehand hit back to be caught by bowler.

2 Make little rallies to each other, emphasizing 'side on' position.

Hoop

1 Bowl to partner while standing or running.

2 Show your partner a favourite way to skip with or balance on hoop.

Group Practices and Small-sided Games
18–27 minutes

Hoop each

Can you make up a sequence that includes 3 different ways to use your hoop, e.g. throw up and catch, walk bowling, skip on the spot in hoop?

Short-tennis in 2s

Throw over rope 'net' (long rope tied between netball posts) for forehand return to partner. A hoop on bowler's side can be target for return strike.

Tunnel-ball rounders

4 or 5 a side. Batting team follow striker to score by reaching 1, 2, 3, 4 cones before fielding team pass ball back through tunnel of legs to end person who calls 'Stop!' Each batter has 1 strike then teams change places.

Games

Teaching notes and NC guidance
Development over 4–5 lessons

Lesson's main emphases:

a The NC requirement to improve the skills of sending, receiving and travelling with a ball in net games.

b Enjoying the variety within summer term Games lessons. In the winter, to keep warm, the games played are nearly all invasion games. In summer we enjoy several versions of racket/net and batting/fielding games; practices with skipping ropes and hoops; and the athletic activities of running, jumping, throwing, hurdling and relays. There should be something for everyone to enjoy.

Equipment: 16 short-tennis rackets and balls; 16 hoops.

Warm-up and Footwork Practices

1 The long hop, the bounding step and the long jump to land on 2 feet are practices that relate to the triple jump. Self-testing across the third of the court will let some of the class learn that they are particularly dynamic as jumpers.

2 Jog, sprint, jog practices can be made more interesting by asking class to count how few sprinting strides they need to cross the middle third. Demonstrate with excellent striders whose thighs are high, and who stride rapidly and long.

Skills Practices: with short-tennis rackets, balls and hoops

1 Practise the individual and partner versions of each piece of equipment before changing to the individual and partner versions of the other one. Hoop on ground activities can include balancing around on feet or feet and hands; hopscotch in and out, as you go around; jumps across; run and jump into; cartwheel in and out. Hoop in hand activities can include skipping; throwing and catching; throwing with backspin; bowling.

2 Emphasise the importance of being 'side on' to partner in racket games so that racket can be at right angles to partner for an accurate straight return. Help partner in learning stages by aiming for partner's forehand side. Try to be stationary at time of hit.

Group Practices and Small-sided Games

Hoop each

Plan a hoop sequence to include 3 varied hoop activities. Aim for a contrast somewhere. For example, 1 action could be very vigorous, as in skipping; 1 on the move as in easy bowling; and 1 slow, where you balance-walk around the hoop on the ground.

Short tennis in 2s

In short tennis over low rope 'net', one throws good length to target hoop or chalk circle. The other with racket returns from a side on to partner position. To encourage care and accuracy the teacher can ask 'What is your best score in good hits for an easy catch before your practice breaks down?'

Tunnel-ball rounders

Limit distance ball is allowed to be hit in tunnel-ball rounders to give fielders a chance to make their tunnel quickly and say 'Stop!' before the batters go all the way around and score 4 points. 'Keep the ball inside this third where we are playing.'

Lesson Plan 10 • 30-45 minutes
June

Warm-up and Footwork Practices
4—6 minutes

1 Run freely, following no-one and hurdling over lines. Which is your leading leg in hurdling?

2 Stand at an angle to a line about 3 steps from it. Can you take a 3-step approach and show me a scissor jump over the line? Start by stepping on to the foot that is your take-off foot.

Skills Practices: with small balls
8—12 minutes

Partner practices

1 Across court, from side line to side line, practise the throwing action from a side on starting position.

2 Now stand closer, about 5 metres apart, with a line mid-way between you. Throw to your partner by way of a bounce on the target line.

3 Stand closer, about 3 metres apart, and throw low (mid-shin) medium (waist) and high (head) to give your partner practice in receiving balls coming at varying heights.

Invent a Game or Practice in 4s
3—5 minutes

Can you invent a game using 1 small ball to develop throwing and catching? For example, 3 versus 1 in circle formation, with '1' in circle.

Group Practices and Small-sided Games
15—22 minutes

Tip-and-run cricket
Batsmen must run to other end when ball is hit. Change duties often if others are slow to get batsmen out.

Hand-tennis, short tennis or quoits
Rope 'net' tied between netball posts (illustrated). 1 v 1. What is your main rule? How many points before changing ends?

Timed team relay
Each team member touches 2 lines and passes baton to next in line. Times of both teams taken several times to record improvement by better turning at ends and baton receipt.

Teaching notes and NC guidance Development over 4–5 lessons

Lesson's main emphases:

a The NC requirements to explore and understand common skills and principles in net and striking/fielding games, to make appropriate decisions quickly and to plan responses.

b A varied content with the athletic activities of running, jumping and relays; striking/fielding skills; and net and striking/fielding games. Those interested in testing themselves in running fast, jumping high, throwing, catching, batting, bowling, fielding, and/or controlling a racket, have plenty to interest them here.

Equipment: 15 small balls; set of wickets or pair of cones; rope 'net' and 10 short-tennis rackets or 5 quoits; 3 relay batons.

Warm-up and Footwork Practices

1 Leading leg in hurdles swings straight up and down. Trailing, following leg bends and lifts around sideways and down to clear hurdle. Action is to run, almost unimpeded, over the low obstacles.

2 In scissor jumps, the foot further from the line being crossed is the jumping, pushing foot. The leg nearer to the line swings up and over the imaginary high jump bar.

Skills Practices: with small balls

Partner practices

1 Throwing about 10 metres across court, start with straight arm behind you in side-on position. Throw by bending and stretching arm with hand coming over shoulder.

2 5 metres apart, with a target line between you, you will still throw overarm to make the ball bounce up well for your partner.

3 3 metres apart only, throw everything underarm with a straight arm action.

Invent a Game or Practice in 4s

The invented game or practice with 1 small ball among 4 should include either a variety of unpredicted angles and speeds at which the ball comes to the catcher, or some form of opposition to impede the thrower.

Group Practices and Small-sided Games

Tip-and-run cricket

In tip-and-run cricket, try to make the receiving batter play at the ball so that both batters must run to change ends. This gives all fielders action and the chance of a run-out or a catch.

Hand-tennis, short tennis or quoits

Play a level of net game which is appropriate for the class: quoits is the easiest, short tennis with rackets the hardest.

Timed team relay

Techniques to speed up the relay include: taking baton while moving forwards; jumping into a turn at each line; jumping into a crouched springing position at each turn; rapid driving steps.

Lesson Plan 11 • 30-45 minutes
July

Warm-up and Footwork Practices
4—6 minutes

1 Run to all parts of the playground alternating between jogging and sprinting, emphasizing: (a) the straightening of the driving leg behind; and (b) the good lift of the leading thigh.

2 With a partner, check how many standing broad jumps your pair needs to travel from side line to side line of netball court. Each starts from previous person's landing spot.

Skills Practices: with small balls
8—12 minutes

Partner practices

1 Stand 10 metres apart. A rolls ball to B who runs forwards, crouches to pick up and return to partner. Change duties.

2 Stand one behind the other. Front partner runs after ball, rolled past him or her gently, stoops to pick up and return to partner. Change places after 6.

3 Stand about 2 metres apart and practise low, medium and high catches. How many can you catch without dropping any?

Invent a Game or Practice in 4s
3—5 minutes

Can you invent a game with 1 ball, emphasizing fielding and catching? For example, 3 versus 1 rounders, where fielders have to make 3 good catches before batter goes around agreed 'diamond' to get batter 'out'.

Group Practices and Small-sided Games
15—22 minutes

Cricket in pairs

Each pair of batters to receive 6 balls, then all change duties by rotating.

Short tennis, 2 versus 2

Rope tied between netball posts. Agree a main rule. When will you change ends?

Athletics circuit

Individual, timed 50 metres sprint. Hurdling over canes on cones. Standing long jump.

Games

Teaching notes and NC guidance
Development over 4–5 lessons

Lesson's main emphases:

a The NC requirement (in athletic activities) to measure and compare results of own performances.

b Hoping that the class will remember their Games lessons with great pleasure, 'an essential by-product of every good Physical Education occasion', and feel inspired to say 'We believe our lessons have been good for us in several ways. We have learned an enormous amount from our teacher and from one another. We are very pleased with and proud of our achievements and our skilfulness. Our class has helped us to get on well together because we have all helped or been helped by others many times. Fresh air and vigorous exercise are good for us, make us look and feel better, and inspire a calmness afterwards.'

Equipment: 15 small balls; rope 'net' and 10 short-tennis rackets; set of wickets or pair of cones and 2 cricket bats; stop watch; 4 canes resting on 8 cones; 1 metre stick.

Warm-up and Footwork Practices

1 If running rhythm is the same, a lifting of the leading thigh to give a longer stride speeds up the running.

2 In standing broad jumps, stand feet apart, toes turned in; swing arms up, down behind with knees bent; throw arms forwards and jump.

Skills Practices: with small balls

Partner practices

1 To field a ball coming towards you, run in and turn as you bend down to put shoulder of throwing arm back. Ball is picked up near front foot and taken back to throwing position.

2 In fielding a ball rolling past you, run beside ball facing same direction, drop to pick up with nearer hand. Take 1 step into a side-on position to put arm behind you into throw position.

3 Standing 2 metres from your partner in a catching practice, have both hands forwards in a 'ready' position. Hands are cupped with fingers forwards, thumbs out to sides. Cup closes around ball to stop it rebounding out again.

Invent a Game or Practice in 4s

Emphasise that ball must stay in agreed, very limited area, which will probably be half of the third in which the group are playing.

Group Practices and Small-sided Games

Cricket in pairs

A group of 8 is the ideal in pairs cricket, with batters having an over (6 balls) in which to score, then all rotating. Agree ways to be 'out'.

Short tennis, 2 v 2

In short tennis, agree the serving method, the scoring system and how many points in a game before changing ends.

Athletics circuit

Circulate in the athletic activities practices: be timed over 50 metres sprint; then you time the next sprinter; have several hurdles practices, trying to lead with same leg each time; then have several standing long jumps, with metre stick for distances.